# Adolescent Growth and Motor Performance

## A Longitudinal Study of Belgian Boys

**Gaston P. Beunen, PhD**
Catholic University of Leuven

**Robert M. Malina, PhD**
University of Texas at Austin

**Martin A. Van't Hof, PhD**
University of Nijmegen

**Jan Simons, PhD**
**Michel Ostyn, MD**
**Roland Renson, PhD**
**Dirk Van Gerven, PhD**
Catholic University of Leuven

**Human Kinetics Books**
Champaign, Illinois

**Library of Congress Cataloging-in-Publication Data**

Adolescent growth and motor performance : a longitudinal study of
  Belgian boys / authored by Gaston P. Beunen . . . [et al.].
    p.   cm. -- (HKP sport science monograph series, ISSN
  0894-4229)
    Bibliography: p.
    ISBN 0-87322-160-5
    1. Adolescent boys--Growth.   2. Motor ability in children.
  I. Beunen, Gaston.   II. Series.
  RJ143.A36  1988
  612′.661--dc19                                                  87-31864
                                                                     CIP

**Managing Editor:** Kathy Kane
**Typesetter:** Angela Snyder
**Text Layout:** Denise Peters

ISBN 0-87322-160-5
ISSN 0894-4229
Copyright © 1988 by Human Kinetics Publishers, Inc.

Printed in the United States of America
3  2  1

**Human Kinetics Books**
A Division of Human Kinetics Publishers, Inc.
Box 5076, Champaign, IL 61820
1-800-DIAL-HKP
1-800-334-3665 (in Illinois)

# Acknowledgments

We would first like to thank, along with our sponsors, directors, and pupils of the secondary schools belonging to the study sample, Prof. Dr. E.J. Willems of the Katholieke Universiteit Leuven and Prof. Dr. P. Swalus of the Université Catholique de Louvain. They both played primary roles in initiating this study and were our team members during the first years of data collection. Furthermore, we gratefully acknowledge the valuable efforts of our secretaries Messrs. L. Van Laer, P. Flour, and M. Teugels, and of our research assistants Dr. A. Claessens, Mr. L. Schueremans, Mr. G. De Beul, Mr. B. Vanreusel, Mrs. L. De Witte, Mr. W. De Vroye, Dr. J. Lefevre, and Drs. R. Wellens who helped us to keep our files up to date and to carry out some preliminary analyses.

Special thanks are extended to Mr. R. Florizoone and Mr. M. Van de Putte of the University Computer Centre, for their advice and most valuable cooperation in computer programming and creation of numerous data files. Without their preliminary efforts this longitudinal analysis would never have been realized. Furthermore, we extend our gratitude to the Matematische Statistische Adviesafdeling of the K.U. Nijmegen for letting us use their computer facilities for the analyses. We are also indebted to the technical and administrative staff of our Institute for their willingness to help us at any time, particularly Mrs. J. Craenen for her care over several typescripts. Moreover, we would like to thank the Bureaus of Statistics and Planning of the Ministry of Nationale Opvoeding and of the Nationaal Secretariaat van het Katholiek Onderwijs. Special thanks in this respect are due to Dr. Jur. A. Van den Bossche.

We also thank the Leuven University Press, and especially Mr. G. Declercq, for permission to let us use parts of the material such as sample description and description of the measurements, already published in *Somatic and Motor Development of Belgian Secondary School Boys*.

Finally, we would like to express our thanks to our very patient sponsors, the Administration of Sport, Physical Education, and Open Air Activities (BLOSO and ADEPS) of the Ministry of Nederlandse Kultuur and the Ministry of Culture Francaise, the Administration of Social Medicine of the Ministry of Public Health, and the Foundation of Medical Scientific Research.

G. Beunen, R.M. Malina, M.A. Van't Hof, J. Simons, M. Ostyn, R. Renson, and D. Van Gerven

# Contents

**Implications**        59

**Summary**        61

# HKP Sport Science Monograph Series

Ten years ago I completed a series of studies on competitive anxiety that validated the Sport Competition Anxiety Test (SCAT). I wanted to publish all this work in one place rather than chopping it into shorter research articles that would meet the space restrictions of scholarly journals. Because a place to publish monograph length research did not exist then in the sport sciences, I published it as the third book of the then neophyte Human Kinetics Publishers.

The need for a research monograph series continues today and was brought back to my attention by Professor Robert Malina when he sought to have the cumulative work of the *Physical Growth and Motor Performance of Belgian Boys Followed Longitudinally Between 12 and 18 Years of Age* published in its entirety. The report of that project is the first publication in the new *HKP Sport Science Monograph Series*. The series is an extension of Human Kinetics Publishers' scholarly journal program.

The *HKP Sport Science Monograph Series* is another endeavor to provide a useful communication channel for recording extensive research programs by sport scientists. Many publishers have discontinued publishing monographs because they have proven uneconomical. It is my hope that with the cooperation of authors, the use of electronic support systems, and the purchase of these monographs by sport scientists and libraries we can continue this series over the years.

The series will publish original research reports and reviews of literature that are sufficiently extensive not to lend themselves to reporting in available research journals. Subject matter pertinent both to the broad fields of the sport sciences and to physical education are considered appropriate for the monograph series, especially research in

- Sport biomechanics,
- Sport physiology,
- Motor behavior (including motor control and learning, motor development, and adapted physical activity),
- Sport psychology,
- Sport sociology, and
- Sport pedagogy.

Authors who wish to publish in the monograph series should submit two copies of the complete manuscript to the publisher. All manuscripts must conform to the current APA *Publication Manual* and be of a length between 120 and 300 doublespaced manuscript pages. The manuscript will be sent to two reviewers who will follow a review process similar to that used for scholarly journals. The decision with regard to the manuscript's acceptability will be based on its judged contribution to knowledge and on economic feasibility. Publications that are accepted, after all required revisions are made, must be submitted to the publisher on computer disk for electronic transfer to typesetting. No royalties will be paid for monographs published in this series.

Authors wishing to submit a manuscript to the monograph series or desiring further information should write to: Monograph Editor, Human Kinetics Publishers, Box 5076, Champaign, IL 61820 for further details.

Rainer Martens

# Preface

Interest in the physical fitness of Belgian youth at the Institute of Physical Education of the Katholieke Universiteit Leuven (K.U. Leuven) dates back to the early 1950s when Michel Ostyn began to direct student theses in this area. This interest soon extended to another initiator of the present project, Jan Simons, who utilized his background in physical education and psychology to develop a motor fitness test battery. Subsequently, a Study Centre for Physical Development of Youth was formed in 1967 at two universities: the Catholic University of Leuven with M. Ostyn, J. Simons, and E.J. Willems as the founding members, and the Université Catholique de Louvain with P. Swalus as the founding member. At this time Roland Renson and Dirk Van Gerven were research assistants and Gaston Beunen was nominated as a research assistant for the study of Belgian boys which comprises this monograph.

The Study Centre for Physical Development of Youth started the Leuven Growth Study of Belgian Boys in 1968. A pilot study was initiated in January 1968 to select the appropriate tests and measurements for physical fitness appraisal in a nationwide sample. Later in 1968 and continuing through 1974, a nationwide combined cross-sectional and longitudinal study was carried out and included more than 21,000 examinations on 8,963 boys 12 through 20 years of age. Observations for each boy included a physical fitness test battery, anthropometric dimensions, somatotype, skeletal maturity, sports participation, and sociocultural characteristics of the family. A description of the project and reference data for all tests and measurements were published in 1980 by the Leuven University Press.

The present monograph is devoted to the longitudinal component of the Leuven Growth Study of Belgian Boys. All measurements were taken at yearly intervals over 6 years in 587 boys between the ages of 12 and 19 years. The somatic and motor characteristics of the boys are first compared to the reference data for the nationwide sample and then changes with chronological age are considered. In order to gain insight into individual variation in growth and performance, individual growth curves for each anthropometric and motor variable are considered relative to the timing of the adolescent growth spurts in height, weight, and static strength.

This monograph is unique in that it is based on one of the largest longitudinal series in which many anthropometric and motor characteristics are studied. In the tradition of several longitudinal studies, the Study Centre for Physical Development of Youth has followed up a percentage of the longitudinal sample who are now adults, and plans to follow this subsample at 5-year intervals. This monograph was prepared while Robert M. Malina was an appointed visiting professor at K.U. Leuven, and with the statistical assistance of Martin Van't Hof.

Gaston P. Beunen
Robert M. Malina

# Introduction

## Growth at Adolescence

Adolescence is a period of transition from childhood to adulthood. Biologically, it is most often viewed within the context of sexual maturation and statural growth. Hence, adolescence may be viewed as beginning with an acceleration in the rate of growth prior to the attainment of sexual maturity and then merging into a decelerative phase, eventually terminating with the cessation of statural growth. The biological events that comprise adolescence are complex. They include changes in the nervous and endocrine systems that initiate and coordinate the somatic, sexual, and physiologic changes; changes in size, that is, the adolescent growth spurt; alterations in proportions and physique; changes in body composition; maturation of the primary and secondary sex characteristics; and changes in the cardio-respiratory system, among others. The biological changes characterizing adolescence are well documented by Tanner (1962, 1970), and for more recent trends in adolescent research see Malina (1978), Chumlea (1982), Sizonenko (1978), Reiter and Grumbach (1982), and Marshall and Tanner (1986). For more detailed analyses of specific tissues and systems see Falkner and Tanner (1986).

## Age Changes and Sex Differences in Motor Performance

Performance in strength and motor tasks is an important item in the behavioral repertoire during adolescence, perhaps more so for boys than for girls (although the relatively recent acceptance of girls in the role of athletes may influence adolescent views and values about their physical performance). Muscular strength is most often assessed in static, dynamometric tests, for example, gripping, pulling, and pushing strength, as in Jones' (1949) classic study. Motor performance is most often measured in a variety of gross motor tasks that require power, speed, agility, coordination, and balance, for example, the standing long jump, shuttle run, ball throw for distance, balance beam walking, and so on.

In boys, muscular strength increases linearly with chronological age from early childhood to approximately 13 to 14 years of age, when there is a marked acceleration through the late teens. In girls, strength improves linearly with age through about 15 years, with no clear evidence of an adolescent spurt. On the average, boys demonstrate greater strength than girls at all ages, though the differences are slight during childhood. The marked acceleration of strength development during male adolescence magnifies the preadolescent sex difference (Asmussen, 1962; Bouchard, 1966, Jones, 1949; Metheny, 1941). With increas-

1

ing age during adolescence, the percentage of girls whose performance on strength tests equals or exceeds that of boys drops considerably, so that after 16 years of age few girls' performance is as high as the boys' average; conversely, practically no boys' performance is as low as the girls' average (Jones, 1949).

Strength is related to body size and muscle mass, so that the sex difference might relate to a size advantage in boys. This is the case only for lower extremity strength. After adjusting for stature variation, sex differences in strength of the lower extremities are not apparent from ages 7 to 17 years. However, from 7 years of age boys are significantly stronger in upper extremity and trunk strength even after adjusting for sex differences in size (Asmussen, 1962).

During growth, strength in both boys and girls increases more than predicted from growth in height alone (Asmussen & Heebøll-Nielsen, 1955). The disproportionate gain in strength is especially apparent during male adolescence. For example, the predicted average yearly increase in strength of a sample of boys followed longitudinally from 10 to 16 years of age was approximately 12%, while the actual average yearly increase was about 23%, or about twice the predicted value (Carron & Bailey, 1974).

These observations thus emphasize the magnitude of the male adolescent strength spurt. The disproportionate strength increase in male adolescence is more apparent in the upper extremities than in the trunk or lower extremities (Asmussen, 1962; Carron & Bailey, 1974). It should perhaps be noted in this regard that the brachial muscle mass practically doubles during male adolescence (Baker, Hunt, & Sen, 1958; Malina & Johnston, 1967).

Performance in a variety of motor tasks improves steadily and markedly in boys through adolescence. The performances of girls, on the other hand, tend to reach a plateau at approximately 14 years of age with little improvement thereafter. Sex differences in motor performance thus become considerable during adolescence. The slopes of the performance trends with age are steep for boys, but are rather flat for girls. In most performance tasks, the average performances of girls fall within 1 standard deviation of the boys' means in early adolescence. But after 14 years of age, the average performances of girls are more than 1 standard deviation below the boys' mean performances. Overhand throwing performance is an exception; few girls approximate the throwing performances of boys at all ages from late childhood through adolescence (Branta, Haubenstricker, & Seefeldt, 1984; Espenschade, 1940, 1960; Haubenstricker & Seefeldt, 1986; Jones, 1944; Malina, 1974, 1980). Jumping and throwing performance in boys shows some acceleration during adolescence, suggesting perhaps an adolescent performance spurt in these power events.

## Maturity-Associated Variation in Motor Performance

During adolescence, biological maturity is related to strength and motor performance. However, the relationships are more apparent for boys than for girls. Correlations between strength and performance, and indices of skeletal and sexual maturation, tend to be moderate in boys (Beunen, Ostyn, Simons, Renson, & Van Gerven, 1981; Clarke, 1971; Espenschade, 1940). The correlations tend to be stronger between 13 and 16 years of age. In contrast, correlations between skeletal and sexual maturity and performance in girls are low, and in many tasks are negative (Beunen, Ostyn, Renson, Simons, & Van Gerven, 1976; Espenschade, 1940). In both sexes, relationships with maturity status are better for static strength than for motor tests. This of course reflects the interrelationships among maturity status, body size, and muscular strength (Malina, 1986a).

The influence of biological maturity-associated variation on physical performance becomes especially pronounced when youngsters are grouped into different maturity categories, that is, early, average, and late maturers, or prepubescent, pubescent, and postpubescent children. And as expected, the differences among contrasting maturity groups are more apparent for boys than for girls. Early maturing boys are stronger than their average and late maturing peers from preadolescence through adolescence (Beunen, Ostyn, Simons, Renson, & Van Gerven, 1980; Carron & Bailey, 1974; Clark, 1971; Dimock, 1937; Jones, 1949). The strength differences between early and late maturers are especially apparent between 13 and 16 years of age, and the strength advantage for the early maturing boys reflects in part their larger body size and muscle mass. When the effects of body size are removed in comparing early and late maturing boys, the strength differences are reduced but not entirely eliminated (Beunen, Ostyn, et al., 1980; Carron & Bailey, 1974). Boys advanced in maturity status maintain their strength advantage.

Early maturing girls are also stronger than their late maturing peers during adolescence (Beunen et al., 1976; Carron, Aitken, & Bailey, 1977; Jones, 1949). The differences are most apparent between 11 and 15 years, and are reduced somewhat by 16 and 17 years of age. The early and late maturing girls thus attain comparable strength levels in later adolescence apparently by different routes. The early maturer shows rapid strength development through 13 years of age and then improves only slightly. The late maturer, by contrast, improves in strength gradually between 11 and 16 years of age. Nevertheless, the differences between contrasting maturity groups of girls are not as great as those between contrasting maturity groups of boys.

Boys advanced in biological maturity status also perform more proficiently in a variety of motor tasks than do less mature boys (Beunen, Ostyn, et al., 1980; Clarke, 1971; Espenschade, 1940). The maturity-associated advantage of early maturing boys is particularly evident in power tasks, for example, the standing long jump, ball throw for distance, and sprints, and is most likely related to the boys' greater muscularity and strength. On the other hand, later maturation in girls is more often associated with better motor performance (Beunen et al., 1978; Espenschade, 1940). For example, in a comparison of high- and low-performing girls, Espenschade (1940) noted that the superior performers were about half a year less mature skeletally and about 5 months delayed in menarche. Similar trends are evident in young women athletes, that is, later maturation is associated with exceptional athletic ability (Malina, 1982, 1983).

## Peak Velocity-Based Changes in Growth and Performance

Adolescence is characteristically variable in timing, intensity, and duration among individuals. To overcome the time spread along the chronological age axis, researchers often align serial data during adolescence on a biological parameter rather than according to chronological age. The most commonly used parameter in growth studies is peak height velocity or maximum increment (Boas, 1932; Shuttleworth, 1937; Stolz & Stolz, 1951; Tanner, Whitehouse, & Takaishi, 1966). Stature and other body measurements are then considered in terms of time before and after the peak height velocity.

Adolescent changes have been considered serially for a variety of measurements relative to the timing of the adolescent height spurt. Pubertal spurts in cranial base lengths, for example, occur prior to peak height velocity in both sexes by an average of 0.3 to 0.8 years (Roche & Lewis, 1974), while a pubertal spurt in bones of the cranial vault occurs coincident with peak height velocity (Lestrel & Brown, 1976). These studies thus document growth in cranial dimensions during the adolescent spurt.

Serial data for biacromial and bicristal breadths aligned on peak height velocity clearly illustrate the development of sex differences in shoulder and hip widths (Marshall & Tanner, 1986), while serial data for a small sample of boys show maximum gains in thoracic and abdominal surface areas coincident with or slightly after peak height velocity (Singh, 1976). Velocities for each trunk surface area are similar prior to peak height velocity, but increments in thoracic surface area are considerably greater during the adolescent height spurt.

Serial body composition data for boys illustrate a peak in lean body mass coincident with the height peak (Pařízková, 1976). However, radiographic measurements of limb muscle and fat widths show a pattern somewhat different from that for the whole-body estimate of lean body mass. When serial data for muscle widths are aligned on peak height velocity, sex differences in the magnitude, and perhaps timing, of the adolescent muscle tissue spurt are apparent (Tanner, Hughes, & Whitehouse, 1981). Boys have a spurt in arm muscle width that is approximately twice the magnitude of that in girls. In contrast, the peak in calf muscle width is only slightly greater in boys. Peak velocities for arm and calf musculature occur after peak height velocity. For the arm it occurs about 3 to 4 months after peak height velocity in boys, and about 6 months after peak height velocity in girls. For the calf, the gain in muscle width appears to be more or less constant from a year or so before to about 1 1/2 years after peak height velocity. Similar data for radiographic measurements of limb fat widths show negative velocities for arm fatness in both sexes coincident with peak height velocity. Velocities for calf fatness also show a trough, but it occurs about 6 months after peak height velocity. However, though the velocities for the boys are negative, those for the girls remain positive (Tanner et al., 1981).

Data relating strength and performance to the timing of the adolescent spurt are limited. Maximum strength development occurs after peak velocity of growth in height and weight in boys, and the relationship is better with body weight (Carron & Bailey, 1974; Stolz & Stolz, 1951). The pattern of maximum strength development in girls is not so clear. The peak of strength development occurs more often after peak height velocity, but there is considerable variation. Moreover, in more than half of the girls the peak strength gain precedes peak weight gain (Faust, 1977).

Only one study has examined motor performance relative to peak height velocity. Ellis, Carron, and Bailey (1975) considered performance in three motor tasks relative to peak height velocity in boys between 10 and 16 years of age. Maximum increase in the standing long jump occurred during and perhaps slightly after peak height velocity, while performance in the flexed-arm hang and bent-knee sit ups showed no clear pattern. Rather, examination of the graphs would seem to suggest that maximum gains occurred prior to peak height velocity in these two tasks.

In contrast to motor performance, several studies have attempted to relate maximal aerobic power ($\dot{V}O_2$ max) to peak height velocity (Cunningham, Paterson, Blimkie, & Donner, 1984; Kemper, 1985; Mirwald & Bailey, 1986; Rutenfranz et al., 1982). Mean ages at peak velocity for absolute maximal aerobic power in Canadian boys and girls (Mirwald & Bailey, 1986) fall between the mean ages at peak velocity for height and weight. Although methods of fitting the data vary among the studies, as do the age ranges encompassed in the samples, results for Canadian, Dutch, German, and Norwegian boys are reasonably consistent. Absolute $\dot{V}O_2$ max begins to increase about 5 or 6 years before peak height velocity and continues to increase through the growth spurt. Relative $\dot{V}O_2$ max is more variable among the four samples, but generally begins to decline a year or so prior to peak height velocity and continues to decline several years after it.

Absolute $\dot{V}O_2$ max also begins to increase in girls several years prior to peak height velocity and continues to increase for several years after peak height velocity in three of the four samples. The exception is German girls, in whom absolute maximal aerobic power does not change relative to peak height velocity. Results for relative $\dot{V}O_2$ max are more variable. It begins to decline 2 to 3 years before peak height velocity in Canadian and German girls, and the decline continues through the height spurt. In Norwegian girls, relative $\dot{V}O_2$ max appears to increase prior to peak height velocity and then begins to decline at about peak height velocity (see also Mirwald & Bailey, 1986).

**Present Investigation**

This monograph reports the growth and performance of a large sample of boys followed longitudinally over 5 years during adolescence. Its general aim is to examine the timing and sequence of adolescent changes in a variety of somatic and motor performance characteristics. To this end, the study proceeded in three stages: (a) a comparison of the chronological age-based distance (i.e., size and performance attained) curves for the longitudinal sample with Belgian reference data to determine its representativeness; (b) a description of the chronological age-based distance and velocity (i.e., change per unit time) curves for somatic and motor characteristics for the longitudinal sample; and (c) an examination of the timing and sequence of adolescent changes in somatic and motor characteristics relative to the timing of peak growth in height, weight, and muscular strength.

The data comprising this monograph are unique in that a large number of both somatic and motor characteristics are considered in a large longitudinal sample. Numbers vary between 270 and 300, depending upon the characteristic that is related to the timing of the spurt in height, weight, or strength. Hence, the data should contribute significantly to the literature on growth and performance. On the other hand, the data comprising this monograph are limited in that only boys are considered, velocities are estimated from annual observations, in contrast to semiannual or quarterly observations which may be more appropriate for adolescent studies and, finally, indices of skeletal and sexual maturation are not included.

# Sample and Methods of Data Collection

## The Leuven Growth Study of Belgian Boys

The Leuven Growth Study of Belgian Boys[1] is a mixed longitudinal study of high school boys on whom measures of physical growth, biological maturity, motor performance, sports participation, and sociocultural circumstances were taken. The study began in 1968 and continued through 1974. A total of 21,175 boys 12 through 20 years of age were examined. The aim of the study was twofold: (a) to describe the current state of physical fitness of Belgian boys at each age between 12 and 20 years, and (b) to gather longitudinal information on the growth of a variety of somatic, skeletal, and motor characteristics, and the sports participation process. A detailed description of the study and reference data for the Belgian population is given in Ostyn, Simons, Beunen, Renson, and Van Gerven (1980).

*Sample.* Considering the number of assistants needed, time available, and costs of such a study, it was decided to examine about 4,000 boys annually over 6 years and thus conduct a cross-sectional and a longitudinal study simultaneously. Since Belgian law obliges youngsters to attend school from 6 to 14 years of age, and nearly all children remain in school until 16 or 17 years of age, it was logical to collect the data in the schools. The study was limited to secondary school boys because adolescence is a period of considerable change in growth, maturation, and physical performance. At the time of the study, most secondary schools in Belgium were not coeducational; hence, only boys are included.

Although children are often examined within 1 or 2 weeks of their birthdays on successive measurement occasions in most longitudinal studies, this was not possible or practical in the study of a nationally representative sample. Thus the boys were examined at yearly intervals during the same period of the school year, starting with the first grade of secondary school (seventh grade in the U.S. system). All measurements were taken during the second school term (January through the first half of April). This alternative approach, whereby individuals are measured at the same time of the year and are selected from different cohorts so that the age distribution covers 1 year, has not frequently been tried in longitudinal studies although it seems to possess some advantages over the usual longitudinal approach (Goldstein, 1978, p. 203).

This study used a multistage cluster sampling procedure. In the first stage, a proportional stratified sample with schools as the primary sampling units was selected. The strata were selected according to the available literature concerning the influence of several factors on the growth and development of body dimensions and motor abilities, the Belgian school system, the language groups, and the geographical distribution of the population. The following four stratification factors were operationalized:

1. Language group—Dutch (Flemish) or French speaking;

---

[1]Parts of this description are adapted from "Chapter I. The Mixed-Longitudinal Growth Study" by J. Simons, G. Beunen, R. Renson, D. Van Gerven, and M. Ostyn. In M. Ostyn et al. (Eds.), *Somatic and Motor Development of Belgian Secondary Schoolboys. Norms and Standards.* Leuven: Leuven University Press, 1980, pp. 11-23.

2. Type of school—vocational or humanities;
3. Private (i.e., Catholic) or state school;
4. Geographical distribution of the school population per province.

After the initial selection was made, other factors such as size of school and population density were considered. This first sampling resulted in the selection of 59 schools. The sampling was carried out by the Dienst voor Statistiek en Planning van het Nationaal Secretariaat van het Katholiek Onderwijs for the Catholic schools and by the Dienst voor Programmatie en Onderwijsstatistieken van het Ministerie van Nationale Opvoeding for the state schools.

In the second stage of the sampling, entire classes were selected from one grade of the secondary school starting with the first (seventh) grade in 1969, the second (eighth) grade in 1970, and so on, until the sixth (twelfth) grade in 1974. The two statistical offices of the Catholic and state schools provided the reference frame of the number of boys to be tested in each school in each year. The secretary of the Study Center for Physical Development of Youngsters, K.U. Leuven, randomly selected a number of classes from each school until the required number of boys was obtained. The total number of boys examined in each grade and testing period is given in Table 1.

Since the same schools were visited each year, it was possible for boys previously enrolled in the study to be selected again the following year. This procedure made it possible to follow a number of boys over several years. Four birth cohorts were measured at six measuring periods, with 5 years of overlapping intervals. Many boys were studied over shorter intervals, while 3,437 boys were measured only once. In this mixed longitudinal design, the total age range varied between 11.5 and 20.5 years.

Table 2 gives the number of boys classified by measuring period and the number of observations. The original sample of 4,278 boys was observed in 1969

**Table 1   Number of Subjects Included in the Leuven Growth Study of Belgian Boys**

| Year | Grade | Number | Testing periods |
|------|-------|--------|-----------------|
| 1969 | 1 | 4,278 | Jan. 13 – May 10 |
| 1970 | 2 | 4,325 | Jan. 12 – March 14 |
| 1971 | 3 | 3,982 | Jan. 11 – March 19 |
| 1972 | 4 | 3,466 | Jan. 10 – March 16 |
| 1973 | 5 | 2,762 | Jan. 29 – March 22 |
| 1974 | 6 | 2,362 | Jan. 28 – March 22 |
|      |   | 21,175 | |

*Note.* From "The Mixed-Longitudinal Growth Study" by J. Simons, G. Beunen, R. Renson, D. Van Gerven, and M. Ostyn, 1980. In M. Ostyn, J. Simons, G. Beunen, R. Renson, and D. Van Gerven, *Somatic and Motor Development of Belgian Secondary Schoolboys. Norms and Standards.* Leuven: Leuven University Press. Adapted by permission.

**Table 2    Number of Boys Enrolled in the Leuven Growth Study of Belgian Boys**

| Measuring period | Number of examinations | | | | | |
|---|---|---|---|---|---|---|
| | 1 | 2 | 3 | 4 | 5 | 6 |
| 1969 | 4,278 | | | | | |
| 1970 | 1,404 | 2,921 | | | | |
| 1971 | 1,287 | 832 | 1,863 | | | |
| 1972 | 1,033 | 727 | 529 | 1,177 | | |
| 1973 | 629 | 604 | 379 | 366 | 783 | |
| 1974 | 332 | 442 | 482 | 239 | 280 | 588 |
| Total | 8,963 | 5,526 | 3,253 | 1,782 | 1,063 | 588 | 21,175 |

See *Note* to Table 1.

when they were in the first grade. Of these, only 558 were followed throughout the 6 years. Such selection was part of the design and can be considered random. However, it should be noted that the boys who were followed on successive occasions were those who had succeeded in their year of school. This may have introduced a systematic bias into the longitudinal samples. However, as shown by Van't Hof, Simons, and Beunen (1980), selectivity in the dropouts did not have a large influence on the measurements.

The present analysis considers only the 588 boys who were followed longitudinally over the 6 years. In order to select the most appropriate data set to test the hypotheses mentioned earlier, the researchers further reduced the number of boys. This reduction and underlying rationale are discussed subsequently in the Data Analyses section.

## Methods of Data Collection

The testing procedure was organized each year as follows. The number of variables to be tested necessitated the creation of two separate teams of trained instructors. One team did all the anthropometric observations, while the other did all the motor tests. Each team consisted of at least 10 instructors, under the permanent supervision of the same three research assistants who accompanied both teams during the entire 6-year period. The three research assistants had practical experience with all tests and measurements, as they had also been involved in the pilot study. The two teams visited selected schools at intervals of 1 week. The subjects were therefore measured by one team during one week, and tested by the other team the following week, and vice versa. A circuit system allowed each team to test a class of 25 pupils within 1 hour. The entire testing program took 3 months per year. The schedule for the testing period was made by the secretary of the Study Center, who visited all schools every year to make the necessary arrangements. During the study, the schools were regularly informed about the results of the study and the activities of the Study Center.

**Table 3   Measurements Operationalized in the Leuven Growth Study
of Belgian Boys**

| | |
|---|---|
| Motor ability tests | Stick balance, plate tapping, sit and reach, vertical jump, leg lifts, arm pull, bent arm hang, 50m shuttle run, 1 min step test. |
| Anthropometric measures | Weight, standing height, sitting height, reaching height, biacromial diameter, transverse chest, biepicondylar humerus, bicondylar femur, chest circumference inspiration, chest circumference expiration, thigh circumference, calf circumference, upper arm circumference flexed, suprailiac skinfold, subscapular skinfold, triceps skinfold, calf skinfold, chest expansion. |

See *Note* to Table 1.

Table 3 summarizes the measurements operationalized in the Leuven Study. The rationale for the selection of the measurements has already been reported (Simons, Beunen, Renson, Van Gerven, & Ostyn, 1980a). Only anthropometric dimensions and motor ability items are considered in this report. Measurement reliability is given in the Data Analyses Section.

*Anthropometric Procedures.*   The measurement techniques stem from a procedure adapted by M. Ostyn, one of the authors, in numerous anthropometric and sports medical examinations. The procedure was based primarily on the description given by Parnell (1958). In agreement with the recommendations made at the International Congress in Geneva (Rivet, 1912), all bilateral measurements were taken on the left side of the body. A description of the anthropometric tech-

**Table 4   Basic Motor Factors and Selected Motor Test Battery
After Factor Analyses**

| Factors identified | Tests |
|---|---|
| 1. Functional strength | Bent arm hang |
| 2. Static strength | Arm pull |
| 3. Explosive strength | Vertical jump |
| 4. Trunk strength | Leg lifts |
| 5. Flexibility | Sit and reach |
| 6. Running speed | 50m shuttle run |
| 7. Speed of limb movement | Plate tapping |
| 8. Eye–hand coordination | Stick balance |
| 9. Pulse recovery | 1 min step test |
| 10. Balance | — |

niques is given in Renson, Beunen, Van Gerven, Simons, and Ostyn (1980) and is summarized in Appendix A.

*Leuven Motor Ability Tests.* The Leuven motor ability test battery (Table 4) was constructed after conducting age–specific factor analytic and reliability studies of a large number of gross motor tests. No balance test was included. At the time of the study, none of the balance tests examined met the reliability criteria. A detailed description of the tests is given in Renson et al. (1980) and also in Appendix B. The factor measured, name of the test, and materials, instructions, directions, and scoring procedure are included in the test descriptions.

# Data Analyses

One aim of this study is the presentation of velocity curves and size- and performance-attained growth curves that are aligned to the moment of the adolescent growth spurt. This implies analysis of individual longitudinal series of observations, which is known to be a precarious concern. The quality of the data is influenced by many factors such as test effects, time of measurement effects, and measurement errors. Further, longitudinal data analyses may be done only after a careful screening of the data. An additional problem in analyzing longitudinal data is the discrete sampling procedure, that is, measurements taken once a year, in a continuous growth process. This section, therefore, deals with the selection of suitable variables and the problem of finding unbiased estimates for growth parameters such as "age at spurt"[2] and growth velocities.

## Models for the Study of Growth Patterns

Growth patterns for a single variable are defined on the basis of the growth velocity curve. Of special interest are the levels of velocities and possible increases in velocity (acceleration) introducing the growth spurt. Several methods have been proposed in the literature for calculating growth velocities. The oldest method includes the analysis of increments. The disadvantage of this approach is that it neglects the continuity of the growth process, which introduces several methodological inconsistencies (see Van't Hof, Roede, & Kowalski, 1976).

A second approach is to fit a preselected equation (growth-function) to the data of a longitudinal series. Growth velocities may then be obtained by differentiation in each selected age point. The issue of concern is the selection of a suitable equation. Many of these functions require a measurement of the final level, that is, adult stature (Marubini, Resele, Tanner, & Whitehouse, 1972). Another disadvantage of this type of analysis is that only "normal" growth curves may be described. In addition, the resulting functional parameters do not necessarily have an easily interpretable biological meaning.

A third class of methods involves the fitting of smoothing polynomials to a longitudinal series. Applications of this method are given by Largo, Gasser, Prader, Stuetzle, and Huber (1978) using cubic splines and Van't Hof et al. (1976) using moving polynomials. The advantage of this method is that no preselected

---

[2]The term *age at spurt* is used instead of age at peak, since the age at peak cannot be exactly defined from measurements taken at yearly intervals (see text for further explanation).

growth model is necessary, since polynomials may be considered as a good approximation of each possible growth function (i.e., Taylor series expansion). A disadvantage of this method is that it requires a high measurement frequency.

Other models for estimating growth spurts are also presented. Marshall (1974) and Tanner, Whitehouse, Marubini, and Resele (1976), for example, used the age at which the calculated velocities show a peak. The biological existence of a sharp peak in the actual growth velocity curve is not certain, however. Children may maintain their maximal growth velocity during a relatively long period. In this context, a plateau model has been developed by Roede and Van't Hof (1979).

It is difficult to directly apply the models discussed above in the present study. The fitting of the well-established growth curves, which are utilized largely for stature and weight, is not promising in this analysis. Data in the Leuven study incorporate a variety of morphological and performance measurements, a limited age range (5 years), and a moderate percentage of boys who reached the adult level. The use of polynomials or cubic splines (for a theoretical discussion see Ahlberg, Nilson, & Welsh, 1967; for a biological application see Van Druten, 1981) is also difficult since there are only six measurement points. It is also difficult to evaluate the fitted curve with respect to its shape with these procedures. This would require the identification of negative velocities, and of local or marginal maximal velocities, which is time consuming in computer programming. The model chosen for the calculation of growth velocities in the present study is thus a compromise that includes the use of polynomials without smoothing and which comes quite close to the increment method.

The identification of a peak velocity or plateau is influenced by a measurement frequency of only one observation per year. It may thus not be possible to distinguish a sharp peak or a longer plateau. Hence, the indication of the spurt is most likely approximate, and it is operationally better to speak of the age of spurt rather than the age of peak velocity or the age of starting the plateau.

Normal biological variation is an additional factor. A clear indication of a height spurt may not be identifiable in longitudinal records for some children, even though measurements are taken at frequent intervals during adolescence.

## Data Screening

Before the actual calculations of velocities and spurts were considered, the data were carefully screened. Several tests were done after Veling and Van't Hof (1980):

1. Data were checked relative to the appropriate range for a specific measurement directly at the time of entering them into the computer. Large errors could be easily detected and corrected.

2. After all the data were collected, consistency checks on the longitudinal series were done. If possible, individual outliers were detected and corrected, or otherwise deleted. As a result of this process, it became clear that the variable "stick balance" was not suitable for further longitudinal analysis.

3. Test effects were detected by comparing boys of the same birth cohort at the same time of measurement and consequently of the same age, but with different numbers of measurements in the study. The anthropometric dimensions did not show any test effect. Among the motor tests, four showed better perfor-

mances by boys having more experience in the study. The four tests were plate tapping, arm pull, leg lifts, and shuttle run. The interpretation of the growth velocities for these variables is thus limited somewhat by the presence of test effects (see Van't Hof et al., 1980).

4. Time-of-measurement effects may be evaluated by comparing boys of the same age who were measured at different times and consequently originating from different birth cohorts. Such a comparison is useful when no cohort effects are present. This assumption probably does not hold in all situations, since the boys were all in the same school grade. Differences in birth cohort may be due to differences in school performance, and probably in maturation and performance of the motor tasks. Therefore, time-of-measurement effects were not analyzed. The mixed longitudinal data analysis proposed by Van't Hof, Roede, and Kowalski (1977) is not useful in this situation, also for the same reasons.

Measurement errors were estimated using data from measurement and remeasurement sessions by an analysis of interperiod correlation matrices (Van't Hof & Kowalski, 1979). Results are given in Table 5. A more detailed description of data processing and screening in this study is reported by Van't Hof et al. (1980).

## Calculation of the Growth Velocities

Although the measurements were taken only once per year, an attempt was made to estimate the velocities for each half year. This includes the calculation of velocities in nine time points ($T_1 \ldots T_9$, see Figure 1). The increments $I_1 \ldots I_5$ were first calculated and corrected for deviations from the 1-year intervals. For instance, the first corrected increment $I_1$ is calculated as

$$I_1 = (O_2 - O_1)/(M_2 - M_1),$$

where $O_i$ = observed value at the ith occasion ($i = 1, 2$); $M_i$ = time of the ith occasion ($i = 1, 2$); and $O_2 - O_1$ is the uncorrected increment, which will not play any role subsequently. The velocities at the even time points ($T_2$, $T_4$, $T_6$, and $T_8$) are calculated, assuming that the growth curve around this time may be described by a second-degree polynomial (parabola). For instance, the calculation of the velocity $V_4$ at $T_4$ is as follows. A parabola is assumed to describe the growth curve $G(t)$ during the time interval of $M_2$ to $M_4$; hence,

$$G(t) = at^2 + bt + c,$$

and the velocity curve $V(t)$ is obtained by differentiation

$$V(t) = G'(t) = 2at + b.$$

This leads to an estimation of the growth velocity

$$V_4 \text{ at } T_4 \text{ of } V_4 = (I_2 + I_3)/2, \tag{1}$$

which is the average value of both surrounding increments. Also calculated in this manner are $V_2$, $V_6$, and $V_8$. More detailed information about these formulas is given in Appendix C.

**Table 5   Results of Screening the Validity of the Variables With Respect to Growth Velocities and Spurts**

|  | Criterion | | | | | |
|---|---|---|---|---|---|---|
| Variable | Correlation initial age $P_{max}$ | Percentage $Q > -0.10$ | Correlation $Q$ and $P_{max}$ | Coefficient of variation $I_{max}$ | Measurement-remeasurement correlation | Presence of test effects |
| Plate tapping | 0.03 | 32% | 0.00 | 33% | 0.63 | + |
| Sit and reach | -0.17 | 13% | -0.09 | 41% | 0.91 | - |
| Vertical jump | -0.08 | 35% | 0.00 | 35% | 0.85 | - |
| Arm pull | -0.12 | 67% | 0.16 | 27% | 0.91 | + |
| Leg lifts | -0.05 | 12% | -0.17 | 48% | 0.68 | + |
| Bent arm hang | -0.04 | 9% | 0.06 | 55% | 0.78 | - |
| Shuttle run | 0.02 | 7% | 0.00 | 84% | 0.68 | + |
| Weight | -0.26 | 89% | 0.27 | 25% | 0.98 | - |
| Height | -0.29 | 96% | 0.75 | 13% | 0.99 | - |
| Sitting height | -0.24 | 77% | 0.33 | 20% | 0.95 | - |
| Reaching height | -0.29 | 77% | 0.44 | 18% | 0.97 | - |
| Leg length | -0.20 | 60% | 0.14 | 26% | 0.94 | - |
| Biacromial breadth | -0.04 | 44% | -0.16 | 27% | 0.84 | - |
| Chest breadth | -0.11 | 50% | -0.05 | 30% | 0.82 | - |
| Biepicondylar humerus | 0.06 | 9% | -0.12 | 38% | 0.88 | - |
| Bicondylar femur | -0.20 | 4% | 0.09 | 39% | 0.73 | - |

*Note.* See text for a more complete description of each criterion.

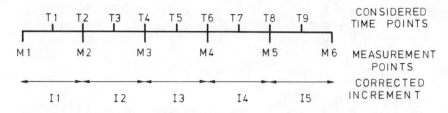

**Figure 1.**  Scheme of the time axis in the study.

The velocities of the odd time points ($T_3$, $T_5$, $T_7$, see Figure 1) are calculated, assuming that the growth curve around this time may be described by a third-degree polynomial. For instance, the calculation of velocity $V_3$ at $T_3$ is as follows. A third-degree polynomial is assumed to describe the growth curve $G(t)$ during the time interval of $M_1$ to $M_4$. Although this assumption is not the same as the assumed parabola around $T_4$, it may be considered consistent because a longer time interval ($M_1$ to $M_4$ instead of $M_2$ to $M_4$) needs a higher degree polynomial, being equivalent to a Taylor series expansion with more terms, in order to obtain comparable precision. This discrepancy in degree was accepted for reasons of symmetry. Thus,

$$G(t) = at^3 + bt^2 + ct + d,$$

and the velocity curve is given by

$$V(t) = 3at^2 + 2bt + c.$$

This leads to the estimation of growth velocity $V_3$ at $T_3$ of

$$V_3 = I_2 + (I_2 - I_1)/24 + (I_2 - I_3)/24, \tag{2}$$

which is the increment of the corresponding interval slightly corrected by information from the surrounding intervals (see Appendix C). Since $T_1$ and $T_9$ have only one surrounding interval, the missing interval is omitted in the formula, that is,

$$V_1 = I_1 + (I_1 - I_2)/24 \text{ and } V_9 = I_5 + (I_5 - I_4)/24.$$

Applied Formula 2 needs explanation. Suppose that $I_2$ is the largest increment, then $I_2 - I_1$ and $I_2 - I_3$ are both positive, resulting in a $V_3 > I_2$. Thus the estimate for the maximal velocity is larger than the maximal increment—an advantage of this method. The maximal velocity is always surrounded by lesser velocities so that the increment containing the maximal velocity is an underestimation of the maximal velocity. The proposed method corrects this bias.

A disadvantage may be that the interval belonging to the largest increment does not necessarily contain the maximum velocity. There is no simple way to correct this phenomenon. A related disadvantage is that the maximum of the estimated velocities always occurs at an odd time point. Suppose that $I_2$ is the largest increment, then $V_3 > I_2$ using Formula 1.

$$V_2 = (I_2 + I_1)/2 < I_2 \text{ and } V_4 = (I_2 + I_3)/2 < I_2$$

since both $I_1$ and $I_3$ are less than $I_2$. Hence, the largest estimated velocity is $V_3$ (or $V_5$ or $V_7$). For this reason, it is not very efficient to calculate the time of the maximal velocity (the age at peak velocity) on the basis of these estimated velocities. A different method had to be developed.

## Estimation of the Spurt Age

An attempt was made to estimate the age of spurt on a half-yearly basis. It is natural to start from the interval having the largest increment ($I_{max}$). Suppose $I_3$ is the maximal increment. The age of spurt may then be assigned to $T_4$, $T_5$, or $T_6$ (Figure 2), depending on the shape of the curve. Two equal surrounding increments form a symmetric situation whereby the spurt age is assigned to the middle (i.e., to $T_5 = 0$ shift). If the preceding increment ($I_2$) is much larger than the following increment ($I_4$), time point $T_4$ is more favorable (i.e., a negative shift). When $I_4$ is much larger than $I_2$, $T_5$ is assigned (positive shift). The decision for a negative or positive shift is made according to the empirical distribution of the shape parameter $S$, defined as the difference between the following and the preceding increment ($S = I_4 - I_2$, in the situation that $I_3$ is $I_{max}$). Considering the half-year basis, the goal is to locate all spurts falling in the interval $\pm 1/4$ year around $T_i$ in $T_i$ (see the arrows in Figure 2). This implies that 25% negative shifts, 50% 0 shifts, and 25% positive shifts must be assigned.

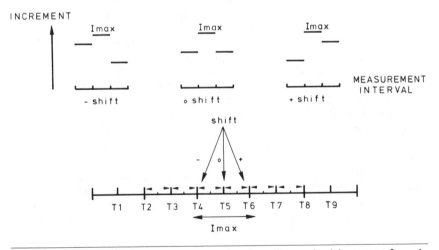

**Figure 2.** Location of the age at spurt starting from the maximal increment $I_{max}$. A negative, zero, or positive shift may be assigned depending on the shape of the velocity curve.

Thus the 25% point and the 75% point of the empirical $S$ distribution are taken as decision points for the shift. In practice, the 25% point is negative and the 75% point is positive. Boys whose maximal increments belong to a marginal interval (i.e., $I_{max} = I_1$ or $I_{max} = I_5$) are excluded from these calculations, first for the technical reason that the shape parameter cannot be computed, and second because a maximal increment in a marginal interval may in fact be submaximal. The implications of this selection are discussed subsequently. It should be noted that the problem mentioned earlier, that is, that the maximal velocity may not be located in the time interval having the maximal increment, is practically solved by this method. The shape parameter in such a situation is so extreme that the spurt age will almost certainly be shifted to the time point where it belongs, taking into account the rounding interval of a quarter of a year.

## Discussion of the Calculation Methods

There are three limitations to the applicability of the proposed estimate of the spurt age. The estimate may be done only for boys having six observations, or for 588 of the initial cohort of 4,278 boys. Due to the measurement procedure in which one day was reserved for the anthropometric dimensions and another for the motor tests, not all 588 boys could be observed in both groups of measurements. Also, incidental observations could be missing for some boys due to problems of data quality. In such a situation the question arises—To what extent is the group of boys with complete measurements representative? This group did not suffer from sickness at the time of measurement, did not emigrate, and was cooperative. Although no significant selectivity in participation could be demonstrated (Van't Hof et al., 1980), the problem of selective participation remains unsolved. ·

The boys having a maximal increment during the first or the last measurement interval were excluded from further analysis. This means that early maturers were excluded. A priori, it is not clear in which direction this selectivity will be most pronounced, but given the age range of the sample, early maturing boys were more likely eliminated than late maturing boys. In order to evaluate the selected group of boys, researchers compared their average growth curve to the average growth curve of Belgian boys (Beunen, Simons, Renson, Van Gerven, & Ostyn, 1980). Independent of this comparison of distance (size- or performance-attained curves), it should be noted that there are several selective restrictions on the longitudinal group so that means and standard deviations in ages at different spurts are not valid for the total Belgian population. Only growth or performance relative to the spurts is meaningful for developmental and for physiological discussion.

The proposed method is valid only when measurement errors are not significant and when the spurts show a classic form, that is, a single increase in velocity followed by a definite slowdown. Further analyses on the basis of the calculated age at spurt may be done only when both criteria are met for a variable. Therefore, a list of validity checks was developed and each had to be met by a variable in order for it to be used in aligning distances and velocities of other variables relative to the age at spurt. The six following criteria were developed:

1. Boys entering the study at an older age (a high initial age) generally must show their maximal increment early in the study, since no relation between initial age and age at spurt is present. This implies a negative correlation between initial age and the rank of the period ($P_{max} = 1, 2, 3, 4,$ or 5) containing $I_{max}$.

2. If measurement errors play an important role, erroneous decreases may occur. This phenomenon is globally checked using the parameter $Q$, defined as the quotient of the minimal and maximal increment, that is, $Q = I_{min}/I_{max}$. The percentage negative $Q$ values must be low. In practice, the percentage value of $Q < -0.10$ is chosen as the criterion.

3. The specific slowdown of growth velocity after the peak introduces the third criterion. If $P_{max}$ (see 1.) is low, there is more time for the slowdown in velocity than for a high $P_{max}$. This implies that parameter $Q$ (see 2.) may be low if $P_{max}$ is low; thus there must be a positive correlation between $P_{max}$ and $Q$.

4. The presence of a real spurt in a variable means an increase in velocity, but there are biological limitations to this maximal velocity. This implies that $I_{max}$ falls in a narrow range. This may be checked by judging the coefficient of variation in $I_{max}$.

5. The importance of measurement error may be read from correlations of replicate measurements as presented by Van't Hof et al. (1980).

6. Since test effects are systematic influences due to regular participation, they will affect growth velocities and also the value of maximal velocity ($I_{max}$). It is not anticipated, however, that the position of maximal velocity (i.e., the age

**Table 6  Evaluation of Anthropometric Dimensions and Motor Tests With Regard to Their Validity for the Determination of a Spurt Age**

| Variable | 1 | 2 | Criterion 3 | 4 | 5 | Final decision |
|---|---|---|---|---|---|---|
| Plate tapping | − | − | − | ± | − | − |
| Sit and reach | ± | − | − | − | + | − |
| Vertical jump | − | − | − | ± | ± | − |
| Arm pull | ± | ± | ± | + | + | ± |
| Leg lifts | − | − | − | − | − | − |
| Bent arm hang | − | − | − | − | − | − |
| Shuttle run | − | − | − | − | − | − |
| Weight | + | + | + | + | + | + |
| Leg length | + | ± | ± | + | + | + |
| Height | + | + | + | + | + | + |
| Sitting height | + | + | + | + | + | + |
| Biacromial breadth | − | − | − | + | − | − |
| Chest breadth | ± | − | − | + | − | − |
| Biepicondylar humerus | − | − | − | − | ± | − |
| Bicondylar femur | + | − | − | − | − | − |
| Chest circumference insp. | ± | + | − | + | ± | ± |
| Chest circumference exp. | − | − | − | + | + | − |
| Thigh circumference | ± | − | − | ± | − | − |
| Calf circumference | − | − | − | + | − | − |
| Flexed arm circumference | ± | − | − | ± | ± | − |
| Subscapular skinfold | ± | − | − | − | − | − |
| Suprailiac skinfold | − | − | − | − | − | − |
| Triceps skinfold | − | − | − | − | − | − |
| Calf skinfold | − | − | − | − | − | − |
| Sum of skinfolds | ± | − | − | − | ± | − |

at spurt) is shifted by test effects. Therefore this check is included primarily for the validity of the velocity curves rather than the age at spurt. The appearance of test effects is based on Van't Hof et al. (1980).

For values related to these six criteria, see Table 5. On the basis of results for the well-established growth variables of stature and body weight, definite critical values were assessed, and are presented in Table 6. Among the linear measurements, stature, sitting height, and leg length (calculated as stature minus sitting height) are the valid measurements with respect to the proposed screening. Weight and arm pull, a static strength test, also met the criteria and were used for further analysis.

## The Study Group

Selected was a sample of 588 boys who were measured at each of the six measurement occasions. Their initial ages varied from 11.0 to 15.0 years. However, the tails of the age distribution were long so that the initial age range was restricted to 11.75 to 13.25 years in order to obtain a reasonably homogeneous group. A total of 510 boys were in this age range initially and were measured six times. There were incidental missing values or missing subgroups of observations for a number of boys, however, so that only 354 boys showed an almost complete set of observations. One of the motor test sessions could not be administered for 67 boys, one of the anthropometric sessions was canceled for 63 boys, while 26 boys showed a high frequency of missing observations. From this group a number were rejected due to an extreme time for the age at spurt. Depending on the variable considered, groups of 270 to 300 boys were available for analysis of data aligned on the age at spurt.

## Further Calculations

The following three types of curves may be drawn:

1. Growth curves: The median growth curves of the group of selected boys (270–300 cases) were calculated in order to evaluate their representativeness relative to the total sample. The size- and performance-attained growth curves were compared to medians (50th percentiles) reported by Beunen, Simons et al. (1980).

2. Growth velocity curves: Median curves were plotted as a reference for growth velocity at different age levels for size and performance variables.

3. Growth velocity curves after alignment to age at spurt: Velocities were plotted relative to age at a given growth spurt. The curves may not serve as reference data, since they are based on a select group of boys. Thus, small errors in absolute measurements may introduce large errors into estimates of velocities. This confounds biological variance with error variance. Further, curves other than the 50th percentile will be estimated as more extreme than they really are, that is, the distance to the 50th percentile is always overestimated.

Two phenomena must be kept in mind when interpreting the curves. First, the assessed test effects in plate tapping, arm pull, leg lifts, and shuttle run (Van't

Hof et al., 1980) overestimate the growth velocities. Second, due to the discrepancy in the method for calculating velocity and spurt age (see Estimation of Spurt Age), the estimated age at spurt may not coincide with the age having the maximal estimated growth velocity. This difference is maximally half a year. Thus, the velocity growth curve of a variable shifted to the age at spurt of the same variable will be flatter than is the case in reality. Velocity curves shifted to the age at spurt of a different variable are not greatly affected by this phenomenon.

# Results

The results are presented in three sections. First, the chronologically based distance, that is, size- and performance-attained medians of the boys followed longitudinally are compared to reference data for Belgian secondary school boys (Simons et al., 1980b). Second, chronologically based distance and velocity curves of the anthropometric dimensions and motor abilities are described. Third, velocity curves for anthropometric and motor characteristics relative to the age at spurt in height, weight, and arm pull strength are given. Also discussed are intercorrelations between the age at spurt and the magnitude of the spurt for the same measurements.

## Longitudinal Distance Curves

Although it is not our purpose to present reference data for the distances and velocities of the different anthropometric dimensions and motor abilities, it is important to evaluate the representativeness of the longitudinal sample. If it can be demonstrated that the longitudinal sample does not deviate markedly from the cross-sectional sample, the conclusions drawn herein may be generalized to the general population. In an effort to conserve space, only a selection of the measurements and tests is considered. For the anthropometric dimensions, the medians for weight, height, biacromial breadth (a skeletal breadth dimension), flexed arm circumference (an indicator of relative muscularity), and the triceps and subscapular skinfolds (fat measurements on the upper extremity and the trunk) were compared with the reference data for Belgian boys. Of the eight motor ability items, two strength tests, arm pull (static strength) and vertical jump (explosive strength), and one speed item, plate tapping (speed of limb movement), were selected for comparison with the reference data.

Although all calculations have been carried out for slightly different samples depending on the measurement that was selected as a reference for the age-at-spurt-based curves, only the curves for the sample used to construct the age-at-height-spurt-based curves are reported. However, it should be noted that the statistical characteristics of the other samples do not deviate from the data presented. Only medians are presented. More detailed information, that is, number of subjects, mean, standard deviation, median, minimum, and maximum values for the size and performance attained in each variable are given in Appendix D, while velocities for each variable are given in Appendix E.

*Anthropometric Dimensions.* The medians for several anthropometric characteristics of the longitudinal series of boys and of the Belgian reference population

**Table 7  Medians of Selected Anthropometric Characteristics in Longitudinal Sample (L) and in Belgian Reference Population (R)**

| Anthropometric characteristics | | Age group (years) | | | | | | | | | | |
|---|---|---|---|---|---|---|---|---|---|---|---|---|
| | | 13.0 | 13.5 | 14.0 | 14.5 | 15.0 | 15.5 | 16.0 | 16.5 | 17.0 | 17.5 | 18.0 |
| Height | L | 151.2 | 153.6 | 156.9 | 160.9 | 165.3 | 169.0 | 171.8 | 173.3 | 174.7 | 175.5 | 176.0 |
| (cm) | R | 153.8 | 156.8 | 160.2 | 163.8 | 167.0 | 169.6 | 171.7 | 173.2 | 174.2 | 175.0 | 175.6 |
| Weight | L | 40.0 | 42.2 | 45.0 | 48.5 | 51.5 | 54.5 | 58.0 | 60.5 | 62.5 | 64.5 | 66.0 |
| (kg) | R | 42.3 | 45.0 | 48.2 | 51.6 | 54.4 | 57.0 | 59.3 | 61.2 | 62.8 | 64.1 | 65.0 |
| Biacromial breadth | L | 32.7 | 33.0 | 33.5 | 34.5 | 36.0 | 37.0 | 37.5 | 38.0 | 38.5 | 39.0 | 39.5 |
| (cm) | R | 33.2 | 33.6 | 34.4 | 35.3 | 36.2 | 37.1 | 37.8 | 38.2 | 38.6 | 39.1 | 39.3 |
| Flexed arm circumference | L | 22.0 | 22.2 | 23.0 | 24.0 | 24.5 | 25.5 | 26.2 | 27.0 | 27.5 | 27.5 | 28.0 |
| (cm) | R | 22.6 | 23.2 | 23.8 | 24.5 | 25.2 | 26.0 | 26.6 | 27.2 | 27.6 | 28.0 | 28.2 |
| Triceps skinfold | L | 186 | 187 | 186 | 185 | 181 | 179 | 172 | 164 | 163 | 166 | 173 |
| (log units) | R | 183 | 183 | 182 | 181 | 180 | 178 | 176 | 175 | 172 | 171 | 170 |
| Subscapular skinfold | L | 157 | 159 | 163 | 165 | 168 | 169 | 171 | 173 | 177 | 180 | 183 |
| (log units) | R | 159 | 162 | 165 | 168 | 172 | 173 | 175 | 177 | 179 | 181 | 182 |

*Note.* From "Norm Scales for Anthropometric Measurements and Motor Fitness" by J. Simons, G. Beunen, R. Renson, D. Van Gerven, and M. Ostyn. In M. Ostyn, J. Simons, G. Beunen, R. Renson, and D. Van Gerven, *Somatic and Motor Development of Belgian Secondary Schoolboys. Norms and Standards*, 1980. Leuven: Leuven University Press. Adapted by permission.

are given in Table 7. The boys of the longitudinal series who show a spurt are somewhat smaller than the reference group up to 15.5 years; thereafter they tend to be somewhat taller in late adolescence. The same trend is apparent for body weight, with the exception that only at 17.5 and 18.0 years are the median values of the longitudinal series somewhat above the reference values. Between 12.5 and 15.5 years the median values for height of the longitudinal series vary between P 34 and P 44 of the reference group; thereafter the medians vary between P 48 and P 53 of the reference group. For weight, the median values range from P 37 to P 44 between 12.5 and 16.5 years, and thereafter they coincide with P 50 of the reference group. However, the maximum differences do not exceed 3 cm for height and 3 kg for weight.

Biacromial breadth of the boys followed longitudinally is slightly smaller than the breadth of the reference group between 12.5 and 14.5 years. After 14.5 years, the curves of the two samples are nearly identical. At the age of maximum difference, the median of the longitudinal group equals P 37.

The P 50 values of flexed arm circumference for the longitudinal series are somewhat lower than those of the reference group over the entire age range. The differences are greater at the younger ages (a maximum difference of 0.9 cm occurs at 14.0 years). At the older ages the curves tend to converge. At the age of maximum difference, the median of the longitudinal group equals P 36 of the reference group.

Medians of the subscapular skinfolds of boys followed longitudinally show the same pattern as those of the reference group. Throughout the age range, the values of the longitudinal group are lower except at the oldest ages. The maximum difference between the median values does not exceed 5 log units, and at this point the median of the longitudinal group equals P 46 of the reference group. The pattern of the medians of the triceps skinfold in the longitudinal sample deviates more from the pattern observed in the reference group. From 12.5 to 15.5 years, the values of the longitudinal series are above the reference values. Thereafter, a somewhat more rapid decline is observed in the longitudinal group, although similar values occur at the oldest age. Between 12.5 and 15.5 years, the maximum difference is 4 log units, and the largest difference between 15.5 and 18 years is 11 log units.

*Motor Abilities.*    The pattern of medians of the distance curves for the two strength tests, arm pull and vertical jump (see Table 8), closely follow the pattern of the reference group. The longitudinal group has somewhat lower values between 12.5 to 15.5 years, but the same or slightly higher values at the older ages. The maximum difference does not exceed 4 kg for the arm pull or 2 cm for the vertical jump. The medians for the age at which the largest differences occur correspond, respectively, to P 39 and P 41 of the reference group.

Speed of limb movement (plate tapping) of boys followed longitudinally is consistently higher than the reference group. The differences tend to increase somewhat from 13.5 to 15.0 years, and then stabilize at about 3 taps per 20 seconds. At this time, the P 50 values of the longitudinal sample vary between P 58 and P 62 for the reference data.

*Summary.*    The sample of boys who were followed longitudinally over 6 years deviates somewhat from the cross-sectional Belgian reference data. The differences occur primarily at the younger ages and then tend to disappear for most

**Table 8   Medians of Selected Motor Characteristics
in Longitudinal Sample (L) and in Belgian Reference Population (R)**

| Motor characteristics | | 13.0 | 13.5 | 14.0 | 14.5 | 15.0 | 15.5 | 16.0 | 16.5 | 17.0 | 17.5 | 18.0 |
|---|---|---|---|---|---|---|---|---|---|---|---|---|
| | | | | | | Age group (years) | | | | | | |
| Arm pull | L | 32.5 | 35.0 | 38.5 | 43.5 | 50.0 | 56.0 | 61.0 | 65.0 | 68.5 | 72.5 | 73.0 |
| (kg) | R | 34.8 | 38.2 | 42.5 | 47.5 | 52.5 | 57.2 | 61.4 | 64.7 | 67.7 | 70.0 | 71.3 |
| Vertical | L | 33 | 35 | 36 | 37 | 39 | 42 | 44 | 46 | 48 | 48 | 47 |
| jump (cm) | R | 34 | 35 | 37 | 39 | 41 | 42 | 44 | 46 | 47 | 48 | 49 |
| Plate tapping | L | 76 | 80 | 83 | 87 | 90 | 91 | 93 | 94 | 95 | 95 | 96 |
| (#/20 sec) | R | 77 | 79 | 82 | 84 | 86 | 88 | 90 | 91 | 92 | 92 | 93 |

See *Note*, Table 7.

measurements near the end of the period under investigation. This would suggest that the longitudinal sample includes relatively more average and late maturing boys than the reference sample. This is due to the selection procedures and sampling techniques used, so that most early maturing boys are excluded from the sample. However, the deviations are not marked, especially in view of the questions that are considered subsequently.

## Chronological Age-Based Distance and Velocity Curves

Median values for distance and velocity curves on a chronological age axis are shown in Figures 3 through 25. As noted earlier, the curves are based on the sample used to construct the age-at-height-spurt curves. Since the distance curves of the longitudinal sample follow the curves of the reference data reasonably closely, only the most salient features of the distance curves are mentioned, and more attention is given to the velocity curves. More detailed information (sample size, means, standard deviations, and median, minimum, and maximum values) is given in Appendix D. For the age-at-spurt-based curves (see Appendix E), only sample sizes, means, and medians are reported, for reasons mentioned earlier in the Data Analyses section.

*Anthropometric Dimensions.* Weight (Figure 3)—The P 50 values increase almost linearly from 12.5 to 16.0 years, followed by a moderate increase. The velocity increases from 3.9 kg/year at 13.0 years to about 6.0 kg/year at 14.0 years. The latter velocity remains unchanged for a period of 1.5 years, and then the velocities decrease linearly.

Height (Figure 4)—Medians increase at a slow rate from 12.5 to 13.5 years and then show a sharp rise until 16.0 years, followed by a gradually attained plateau. In contrast to the weight velocity curve, median velocities for height show a clear spurt even on a chronological age base. Starting from a velocity of 5.1 cm/year at 13.0 years, the medians increase to 8.0 cm/year at 14.5 years, followed by a gradual decrease to about 1.3 cm/year at 17.5 years.

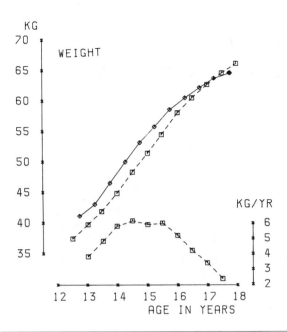

**Figure 3.** Chronological age-based distance and velocity curves for body weight in the longitudinal sample ( ⊡– – – –⊡ ).

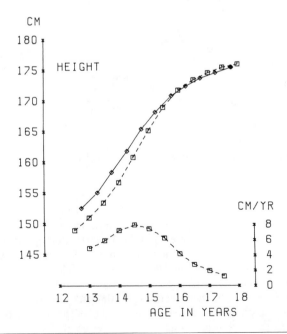

**Figure 4.** Chronological age-based distance and velocity curves for height in the longitudinal sample ( ⊡– – – –⊡ ).

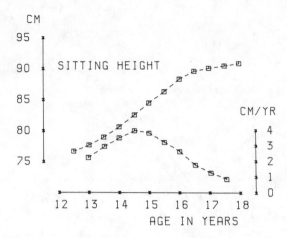

**Figure 5.**   Chronological age-based distance and velocity curves for sitting height.

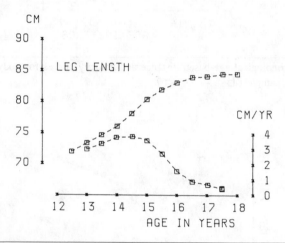

**Figure 6.**   Chronological age-based distance and velocity curves for leg length.

Sitting height and leg length (Figures 5 and 6)—The distance curve of sitting height displays a sharp increase between 13.5 and 16.0 years, followed by a plateau. The increase in leg length is almost linear from 12.5 to 15.5 years. A spurt is visible for both measurements at 14.5 years, although it is clearer for sitting height than for leg length. Median velocities for sitting height increase from 2.3 cm/year to 4.0 cm/year, and then decrease to 0.9 cm/year at 17.5 years. For leg length, the velocity at 13.0 years is about 3.0 cm/year, increasing to 3.8 cm/year at 14.5 years, and then declining to 0.4 cm/year at 17.5 years.

Biacromial and chest breadths (Figures 7 and 8)—The largest increase in the medians of the two trunk dimensions occurs between 14.5 to 15.0 and 15.0 to 15.5 years, respectively, after which a smaller increase is observed. The velocity curve of biacromial breadth increases from 0.4 cm/year at 13.0 years to about 2.1 to 2.2 cm/year at 14.5 and 15.0 years. The velocities stabilize from 16.0

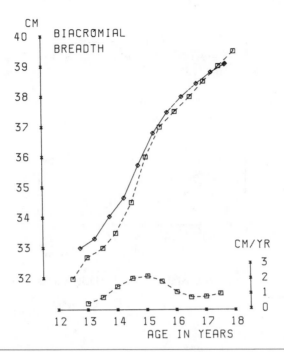

**Figure 7.** Chronological age-based distance and velocity curves for biacromial breadth in the longitudinal sample ( ▭– – – –▭ ).

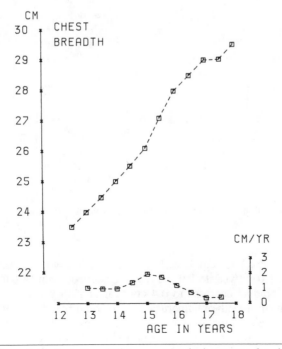

**Figure 8.** Chronological age-based distance and velocity curves for chest breadth.

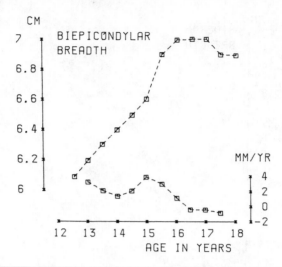

**Figure 9.** Chronological age-based distance and velocity curves for biepicondylar breadth of humerus.

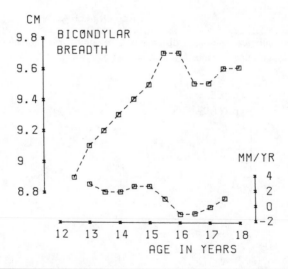

**Figure 10.** Chronological age-based distance and velocity curves for bicondylar breadth of femur.

to 17.5 years at about 1.0 cm/year. For chest breadth, only a slight increase in velocities from 1.0 cm/year to 1.9 cm/year is observed, from 14.0 to 15.0 years, followed by a gradual decrease to 0.4 cm/year at 17.5 years.

Biepicondylar breadth of humerus and bicondylar breadth of femur (Figures 9 and 10)—The medians for size attained increase almost linearly until 15.0 years, while a sharper increase over a shorter period is subsequently observed in both extremity breadths. At the upper limit of the age range an irregular pattern oc-

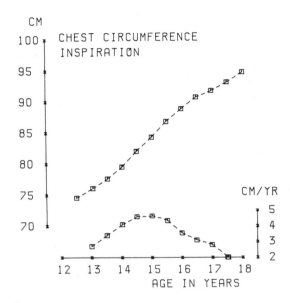

**Figure 11.**   Chronological age-based distance and velocity curves for chest circumference inspiration.

curs, most probably reflecting measurement variability. The biepicondylar velocities decline from about 2.5 to 1.5 mm/year between 13.0 and 14.0 years, and then increase to 3.9 mm/year by 15.0 years. Between 16 and 16.5 years, the velocities become negative. The velocities of femoral bicondylar breadth show a small decrease from 2.9 mm/year to 2.0 mm/year between 13.0 and 14.0 years, then an increase to 2.8 mm/year by 15.0 years. Between 16.5 and 17.0 years, negative velocities are apparent. The negative velocities most likely reflect measurement variability, but soft tissue changes over the condyles may also be a factor in both extremity breadth measurements.

Chest circumference at inspiration (Figure 11)—Only one chest circumference measurement is discussed, although similar results are apparent for the three measurements taken. There is a linear increase from 12.5 to 16.5 years, and the velocity curve shows a maximum at 14.5 to 15.0 years. The velocities increase from 2.7 cm/year at 13 years to 4.7 cm/year at 14.5 and 15.0 years, and then decrease to 1.9 cm/year at 17.5 years.

Flexed arm, thigh, and calf circumferences (Figures 12, 13, and 14)—Median distance values of the three limb circumferences show a linear increase from 13.0 to 18.0 years. The velocities increase from 13.0 to 14.0 years, followed by a plateau, and then decline. Maximum velocities are 1.5 cm/year for flexed arm and calf circumferences, and 2.5 cm for thigh circumference.

Subscapular and suprailiac skinfolds (Figures 16 and 17)—Skinfold measurements taken at trunk sites increase from 12.5 to 18.0 years. Velocities for the subscapular skinfold are rather constant from year to year, showing a slight decrease from 14.5 to 16.0 years, while those for the suprailiac skinfold decrease gradually from 13.5 to 16.0 years, and then decline markedly, showing negative values at 17.0 years.

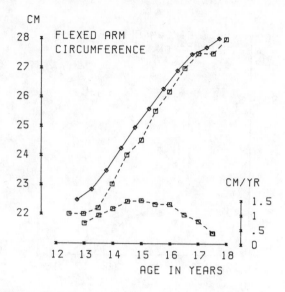

**Figure 12.** Chronological age-based distance and velocity curves for flexed arm circumference in the longitudinal sample ( □─ ─ ─ ─□ ).

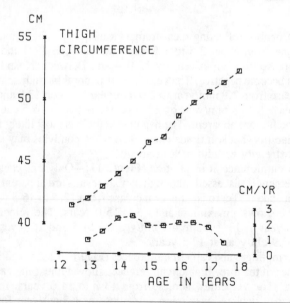

**Figure 13.** Chronological age-based distance and velocity curves for thigh circumference.

Triceps and calf skinfolds (Figures 15 and 18)—The trends of the distance curves for these two extremity skinfolds are quite different from each other and from the trunk skinfolds. The triceps skinfold decreases over the entire age period, while the calf skinfold increases from 12.5 to 15.0 years and then decreases.

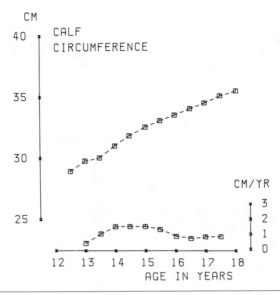

**Figure 14.** Chronological age-based distance and velocity curves for calf circumference.

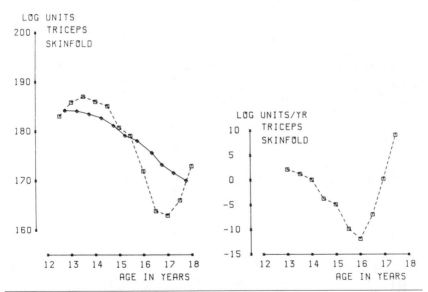

**Figure 15.** Chronological age-based distance and velocity curves for triceps skinfold in the longitudinal sample ( ▫─ ─ ─ ─▫ ).

Velocities for triceps skinfold are negative except at each end of the age range. A minimum of −12 log units/year occurs at 16.0 years. For the calf skinfold, velocity is maximal (9 log units/year) at 14.0 years and then declines linearly, becoming negative between 14.5 and 15.0 years. A minimum value of −22 log units/year occurs at 17.5 years.

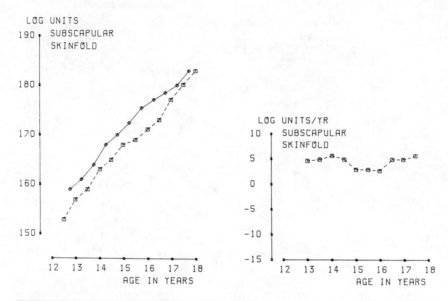

**Figure 16.** Chronological age-based distance and velocity curves for subscapular skinfold in the longitudinal sample ( ▫− − − −▫ ).

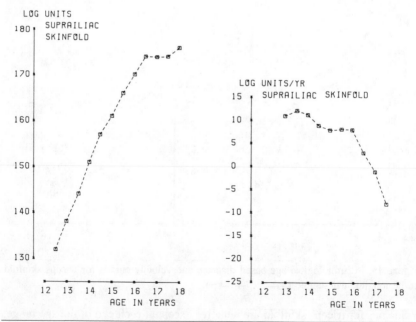

**Figure 17.** Chronological age-based distance and velocity curves for suprailiac skinfold.

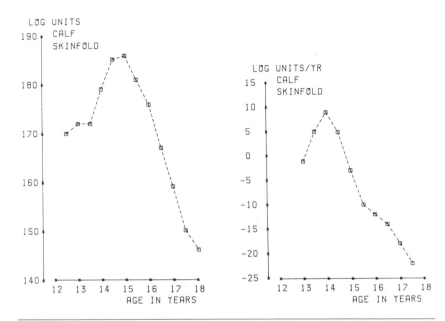

**Figure 18.**    Chronological age-based distance and velocity curves for calf skinfold.

*Motor Abilities.*    Static and explosive strength (arm pull and vertical jump, Figures 19 and 20)—The two strength measurements increase linearly and the largest increases occur between 14.0 or 14.5 and 17.0 years. Static strength (arm pull) continues to increase after 17.0 years, while explosive strength (vertical jump) reaches a plateau at this age. Both velocity curves show a clear maximum at 15.0 years. Velocities of static strength increase from 4.9 kg/year to 11.9 kg/year, and then decrease to 6.5 kg/year. Velocities for explosive strength increase from 2.7 cm/year to 4.5 cm/year, and then decrease to 1.4 cm/year.

Functional strength (bent arm hang, Figure 21)—This strength test also shows considerable increase in performance from 12.5 to 16.0 years, with an apparent plateau at the older ages. Velocities increase from 2.2 sec/year at 13.0 years to 5.5 sec/year at 15.5 years, followed by a decline which becomes negative ($-1.4$ sec/year) at 17.5 years.

Trunk strength (leg lifts, Figure 22)—The increase in this strength task is rather limited and discrete in the longitudinal sample. In contrast, the medians increase continuously in the reference sample. As such, the velocities show an odd pattern, fluctuating between 0 and 1 lift/year. Maximal values are found at 14.0, 14.5, and 17.5 years. The limited age change in this task may be a function of the scoring system, that is, performance was scored in whole units only as complete lifts.

Speed of limb movement (plate tapping, Figure 23)—Speed of limb movement increases almost linearly between 12.5 and 16.5 years, followed by a plateau. The velocity curve begins with a plateau (6.8 to 7.0 taps/year) and then gradually declines until 16.0 years and levels off (2.6 to 2.7 taps/year).

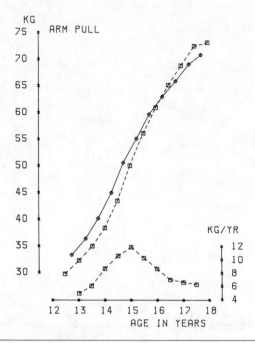

**Figure 19.** Chronological age-based distance and velocity curves for arm pull in the longitudinal sample ( □— — — —□ ).

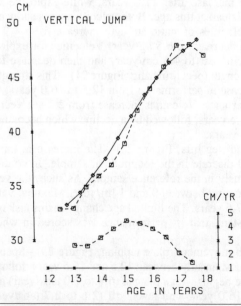

**Figure 20.** Chronological age-based distance and velocity curves for vertical jump in the longitudinal sample ( □— — — —□ ).

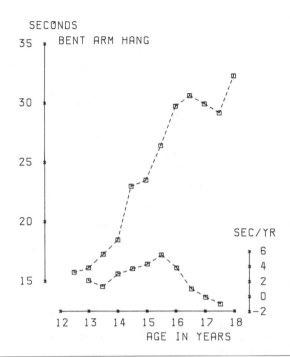

**Figure 21.** Chronological age-based distance and velocity curves for bent arm hang.

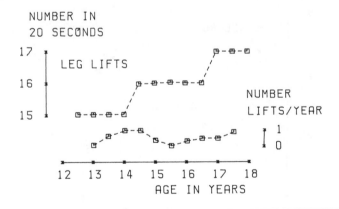

**Figure 22.** Chronological age-based distance and velocity curves for leg lifts.

Running speed (shuttle run, Figure 24)—The scale of the ordinate is reversed for the run, since a better performance is reflected by a lower time. Performance increases from 12.5 to 17.5 years. Although the pattern of the velocity curve is somewhat irregular, a general decrease in velocity is observed between 13.0 and 17.5 years. The values range from 0.7 sec/year to 0.2 sec/year.

Flexibility (sit and reach, Figure 25)—Although a smooth, continuous increase in this test is apparent in the reference data, the longitudinal medians display several plateaus. In general, however, performances increase from 13.0 until

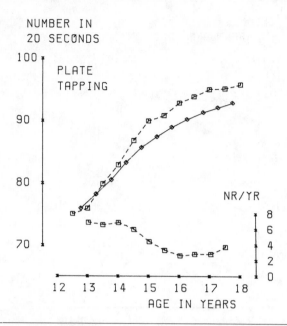

**Figure 23.** Chronological age-based distance and velocity curves for plate tapping in the longitudinal sample ( □─ ─ ─ ─ ─□ ).

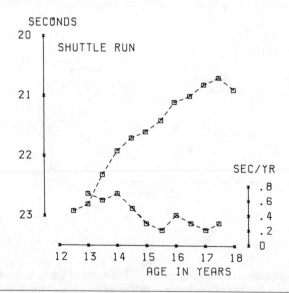

**Figure 24.** Chronological age-based distance and velocity curves for shuttle run.

17.5 years, and the velocities fluctuate between 0.9 cm/year and 1.0 cm/year over the age range.

***Summary.***    With the exception of skinfolds on the extremities, all anthropometric dimensions increase during adolescence. Weight and all lengths, trunk breadths,

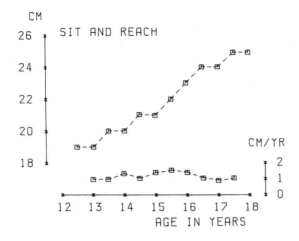

**Figure 25.** Chronological age-based distance and velocity curves for sit and reach.

and circumferences show a maximum velocity between 14.0 and 15.0 years. A plateau, rather than a clear peak, is apparent for weight and the flexed arm and calf circumferences. No real peak or plateau is apparent for the bone breadths. Velocities of the suprailiac skinfold decline gradually over adolescence, while they are generally stable for the subscapular skinfold. Velocities for the triceps skinfold rapidly become negative and show a minimum at 16 years. A maximum velocity for the calf skinfold occurs at 14.0 years, and then the velocities become negative.

Performances in all motor fitness items increase during adolescence. The increase in trunk strength (leg lifts) is rather small. The velocity curves of the three strength tasks, static (arm pull), explosive (vertical jump), and functional strength (bent arm hang), show a reasonably clear peak. The velocities for running speed (shuttle run) and speed of limb movement (plate tapping) gradually decline after 13.0 or 14.0 years, while those for trunk strength (leg lifts) and flexibility (sit and reach) remain stable.

### Age-at-Spurt-Based Distance and Velocity Curves

Since chronological age-based velocities tend to underestimate the maximum velocity due to the time-spreading effect (Shuttleworth, 1937; Tanner, 1951), velocity curves of the anthropometric dimensions and motor abilities are plotted against the age at spurt of different measurements. Only several variables are valid for a definition of the age at spurt and the spurt itself. Thus, it is not possible to construct age-at-spurt-based distance and velocity curves for each variable against its own age at spurt. Such age-at-spurt-based curves could be constructed only for those measurements that met the selection criteria (see Table 6 in Data Analyses section). These include weight, height, reaching height, sitting height, leg length, chest circumference at inspiration, and static strength (arm pull).

To avoid redundancy and complication, only the age at spurt in height, weight, and static strength (arm pull) are used as the time scales. Height and weight are the most commonly used anthropometric dimensions in growth studies, and the three other anthropometric dimensions that meet the imposed criteria are length measurements, which are highly interrelated with height. Furthermore, ages at peak velocities of length measurements are also highly interrelated (Tanner et al., 1976). Although chest circumference at inspiration meets the imposed criteria, it is marginal for some of the criteria. On the other hand, arm pull, which is also marginal for some of the criteria, is the most valid motor ability test for the definition of the age at spurt and the spurt itself. Hence, it was retained for the analysis. The ranges of the number of subjects available at each half year before and after the spurts in height (HS), weight (WS), and arm pull (APS)[3] are given in Table 9.

**Table 9   Number of Subjects at Successive Half-Year Intervals Before and After Age at Height Spurt (HS), Weight Spurt (WS), and Arm Pull Spurt (APS)**

| −2.5 | −2.0 | −1.5 | −1.0 | −0.5 | 0 |
|---|---|---|---|---|---|
| 33–42 | 78–101 | 141–187 | 196–256 | 210–276 | 210–276 |
| 79–102 | 112–145 | 150–199 | 198–263 | 219–291 | 219–291 |
| 67–87 | 120–156 | 180–229 | 226–288 | 236–301 | 236–301 |

| +0.5 | +1.0 | +1.5 | +2.0 | +2.5 | +3.0 |
|---|---|---|---|---|---|
| 210–276 | 210–276 | 210–276 | 212–275 | 202–263 | 177–234 |
| 219–291 | 219–291 | 219–291 | 213–283 | 182–242 | 140–189 |
| 236–301 | 236–301 | 236–301 | 231–295 | 210–270 | 169–214 |

*Note.* Exact number of subjects varies with each variable.

***Anthropometric Dimensions.***    Weight (Figure 26)—The WS-based velocities increase from 3.6 kg/year at 2.5 and 2.0 years before WS until 7.9 kg/year at WS, and then decline rapidly to 3.4 kg/year at 1.5 years after WS, followed by a gradual tapering. A clearer spurt in body weight is more apparent in the curve based on WS than in the one based on HS, and it is about 1 kg/year higher. There is also a tendency for the maximum gain to occur later relative to HS, since the velocity at 0.5 year after HS (6.7 kg/year) is slightly higher than the velocity at 0.5 year before HS (6.4 kg/year).

Height (Figure 26)—Velocities increase from 3.9 cm/year at 2.0 years before HS to a maximum of 8.7 cm/year at HS. The maximum height velocity for the WS-based curve is 0.8 cm/year lower than HS-based estimates. Moreover, the maximum velocity of height in the WS curve precedes the zero point, indicating that HS occurs before WS.

---

[3]To avoid repetition, height spurt, weight spurt, and arm pull spurt are abbreviated as follows: HS, WS, and APS, respectively.

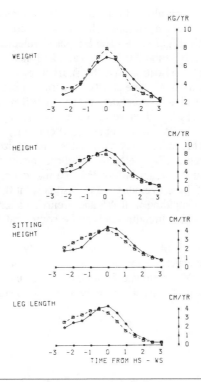

**Figure 26.** Age-at-spurt-based velocity curves for body weight and length measurements aligned on height spurt ( ▫——————▫ ) and weight spurt ( ▫— – – —▫ ).

Sitting height (Figure 26)—The HS-based velocities increase from 1.8 cm/year to 4.4 cm/year at the maximum. The decrease in velocity after HS is slightly slower than the increase. The velocity of growth in sitting height at 0.5 years after HS (4.2 cm/year) is greater than the velocity at 0.5 years before HS (3.8 cm/year). This would suggest that the spurt in sitting height occurs somewhat later than the spurt in height itself.

An opposite trend is apparent in the WS-based curve, indicating that the spurt in sitting height precedes WS. Further, the maximum velocity of the WS-based curve is slightly less (4.1 cm/year) than for the HS-based curve, which indicates that the synchronization of the spurt in sitting height is somewhat better when aligned on HS than on WS.

Estimated leg length (Figure 26)—Velocities increase from 2.0 cm/year at 2.5 years before HS to 4.3 cm/year at HS, decrease to 1.3 cm/year at 1.5 years after HS, and then gradually decline to 0.3 cm/year. There is no difference in the maximum velocities of leg length (4.3 cm/year) and sitting height (4.4 cm/year). Since the velocity of growth in leg length at 0.5 years before HS (4.1 cm/year) is larger than the velocity at 0.5 years after HS (3.6 cm/year), the spurt in leg length clearly precedes HS. Further, the spurt in leg length precedes WS by about 0.5 years. As for sitting height, the synchronization of the growth spurt in leg length is better when aligned on HS (maximum velocity is 4.3 cm/year) than when aligned on WS (maximum velocity is 3.9 cm/year).

Biacromial breadth (Figure 27)—The HS-based velocities are constant from 2.5 to 1.5 years before HS (about 0.5 cm/year), and increase to 2.3 cm/year at HS. There is also some indication that the spurt in biacromial breadth occurs after HS. When aligned on WS, the spurt in biacromial breadth coincides more with WS (velocities at 0.5 before and 0.5 years after WS are identical). The maximum velocity on the HS-based curve (2.3 cm/year) is slightly higher than the maximum velocity on the WS-based curve (2.0 cm/year), which suggests that the spurt in biacromial breadth is somewhat better synchronized with HS than WS.

Chest breadth (Figure 27)—Velocities of chest breadth increase only slightly from 0.5 cm/year at 2.0 years before HS to a maximum of 1.7 cm/year 0.5 year after HS. The WS-based velocity curve is somewhat flatter, with maximum chest breadth velocity coinciding with WS and occurring after HS. The synchronization of the spurt in chest breadth tends to be somewhat better when aligned on HS than on WS.

Biepicondylar breadth of the humerus and bicondylar breadth of the femur (Figure 27)—Both skeletal breadths of the extremities show rather flat velocity curves prior to HS or WS, followed by a tapering of velocities after the spurt. A small peak seems to be apparent for the two measurements at 1.0 year before

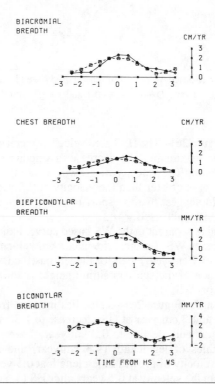

**Figure 27.** Age-at-spurt-based velocity curves for skeletal breadths aligned on height spurt ( □————□ ) and weight spurt ( □– – – –□ ).

WS, while only biepicondylar breadth of the humerus shows a small peak 0.5 year after HS.

Chest circumference at inspiration (Figure 28)—Velocities aligned on HS increase linearly from 1.9 cm/year at 2.5 years before HS to 5.1 cm/year at HS and 0.5 year after HS, and then decrease linearly to about 2.0 cm/year at 2.5 years after HS. When aligned on WS, the velocities are similar, but the peak occurs slightly earlier, that is, 0.5 year before and at WS. Thus the spurt in chest circumference probably occurs just after HS and just before WS.

Flexed arm circumference (Figure 28)—Velocities increase from 0.4 cm/year to 1.7 cm/year at HS, and then slowly decrease to a value of 1.4 cm/year 1.5 years after HS. The velocities subsequently decline to 0.4 cm/year. WS-based velocities increase from 0.5 cm/year to 2.0 cm/year at WS, and then decline rapidly to 0.9 cm/year at 1.5 years after WS.

Thigh circumference (Figure 28)—HS-based velocities increase from 0.4 cm/year at 2.5 years before HS to 2.4 cm/year at 0.5 year before and at HS. The velocities then decrease gradually to a value of 1.9 cm/year 2.5 years after HS. WS-based velocities show a clearer spurt of 3.0 cm/year coincident with WS. The spurt in thigh circumference tends to occur just before HS and then remains flat. On the other hand, the spurt in thigh circumference clearly coincides with WS. WS ordinarily follows HS so that the trend in thigh circumfer-

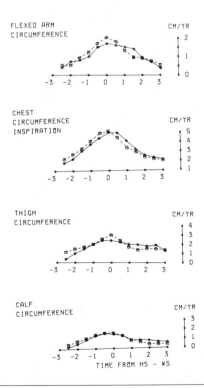

**Figure 28.**   Age-at-spurt-based velocity curves for circumferences aligned on height spurt ( ▫——————▫ ) and weight spurt ( ▫— – – —▫ ).

ence may possibly reflect sampling variation. For the HS-based data, the sample is 269, and the minimum and maximum velocities at HS are, respectively, −6.8 cm/year and +8.7 cm/year. For the WS-based curves, the sample is 282, and the minimum and maximum velocities at WS are, respectively, −1.5 cm/year, and +8.7 cm/year. Further confounding factors are adolescent fat loss (see below) and measurement variability.

Calf circumference (Figure 28)—The HS- and WS-based velocity curves are nearly identical. A maximum velocity of 1.7 cm/year is attained at 0.5 year before HS, and at 0.5 year before and at WS. The spurt in calf circumference thus tends to precede HS and WS, but probably occurs closer to WS. It should be noted that fat tissue is included in the measurement, and there is a marked decrease in calf fat at or immediately after HS and WS (see below).

Triceps skinfold (Figure 29)—The velocities show positive values until 1.0 year before HS and 1.5 years before WS. For both curves, a minimum velocity of −8 log units/year occurs 1.5 years after HS and WS. Subsequent velocities increase and become positive. Thus, during the height and weight spurts, boys absolutely lose fat over the triceps muscle of the upper arm.

Calf skinfold (Figure 29)--Both HS- and WS-based velocity curves for the calf skinfold are quite similar. Both show a peak 2.0 years before HS and WS. Subsequently, the velocities decline linearly, become negative at WS and HS,

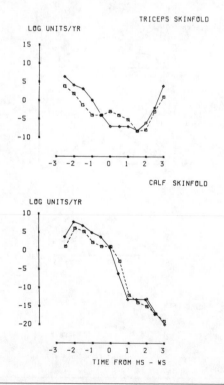

**Figure 29.** Age-at-spurt-based velocity curves for extremity skinfolds aligned on height spurt ( ▫――――▫ ) and weight spurt ( ▫– – – –▫ ).

and continue to be negative, reaching −20 log units/year 3.0 years after the spurts.

Subscapular skinfold (Figure 30)—In contrast to the extremity skinfolds, velocities of the subscapular skinfold remain positive throughout the adolescent spurt. Velocities fluctuate between 2 log units/year and 7 log units/year.

Suprailiac skinfold (Figure 30)—Velocities increase from 9 log units/year 2.5 years before HS until 12 log units/year 1.0 year before HS. Velocities then decline, at first gradually to 10 log units/year at 0.5 year after HS, and then quite rapidly to −4 log units/year 3.0 years after HS. The WS-based velocities increase from 9 log units/year 2.5 years before WS to 14 log units/year at WS, and then decline rapidly to −7 log units/year 3.0 years after the spurt.

*Motor Abilities.*    Each motor fitness item is considered relative to HS and WS. In addition, each task is considered relative to the spurt in static strength as expressed in the arm pull spurt (APS).

Static strength (arm pull, Figure 31)—The APS-based velocity curve for static strength decreases slightly from 7.1 kg/year at 2.5 years to 5.7 kg/year 1.5 years before the spurt, and then increases rapidly to 15.0 kg/year at APS. Subsequently, this strength velocity decreases dramatically to 4.4 kg/year 1.5 years after APS. Thus the pubertal spurt in static strength occurs over 3 years (1.5 years before to 1.5 years after APS). Both the HS- and WS-based velocity curves for

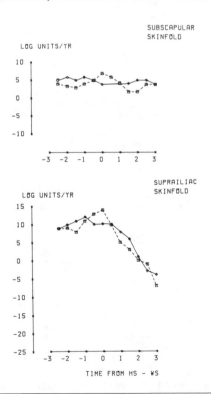

**Figure 30.**  Age-at-spurt-based velocity curves for trunk skinfolds aligned on height spurt ( □————□ ) and weight spurt ( □− − − −□ ).

static strength do not show such a dramatic adolescent spurt. The maximum reaches 12.1 kg/year 0.5 year after HS, and 11.2 kg/year at WS and 0.5 year after WS. The HS clearly precedes APS, while WS tends to precede APS. The spurt in arm pull strength is similar when aligned on HS or WS, but somewhat better for the former.

Explosive strength (vertical jump, Figure 31)—The HS-based velocities for the vertical jump increase from 2.0 cm/year 1.5 years before HS to 4.8 cm/year at 0.5 year after HS, and then decline linearly to 2.0 cm/year 3.0 years after HS. The velocity curves based on WS and APS are similar in shape and are quite flat compared to the HS-based curve. A maximum vertical jump velocity of 4.2 cm/year is apparent for the WS- and APS-based curves. The spurt in the vertical jump follows the HS by about 0.5 year, and appears coincident with WS and APS.

Functional strength (bent arm hang, Figure 31)—The HS-based velocities decline from 0.9 sec/year to 0.3 sec/year 1.5 years before HS, and then increase to a maximum plateau of 4.9 sec/year at HS through 1.0 year after HS. Subsequently, a rapid decline occurs with negative velocities apparent 2.5 and 3.0 years after HS. The WS-based curve is flatter than the HS-based curve, and also shows a plateau from 0.5 year before through 1.0 year after WS. A similar decline as noted for the HS-based curve then follows. The APS-based data for the bent arm

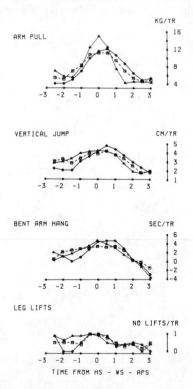

**Figure 31.** Age-at-spurt-based velocity curves for strength measurements aligned on height spurt ( ▫————▫ ), weight spurt ( ▫— – – —▫ ), and arm pull spurt ( △— – – —△ ).

hang show a more defined spurt, with a linear increase from 1.5 sec/year 2.0 years before to 5.1 sec/year at APS. After the spurt, velocities decrease and eventually become negative. Thus the spurt in bent arm hanging performance tends to coincide with APS and to follow HS and WS.

Trunk strength (leg lifts, Figure 31)—Velocities for this measure of trunk strength vary between 0 and 1.0 lift/year, with no evidence of a spurt. However, the highest velocities occur around the time of HS, WS, or APS, followed by a gradual decline to zero.

Speed of limb movement (plate tapping, Figure 32)—The velocity curves aligned on HS, WS, and APS decrease linearly from about 6 to 8 taps/year 2.5 to 2.0 years before the spurts to about 2 taps/year 2.0 years after the spurts. Thus, if there is a spurt in the speed of limb movement as measured by this task, the trends suggest that it occurs at least 2.5 years before HS, WS, or APS.

Running speed (shuttle run, Figure 32)—Maximum velocities of about 0.7 sec/year occur 2.0 to 1.0 year before the respective spurts, followed by a decline until 1.5 years after HS, WS, or APS. There appears to be a small increase in velocities 2.5 to 3.0 years after the spurts. Thus, for running speed, evidence suggests that a spurt in performance, if there is one, occurs about 2 years before the HS, WS, or APS. It should also be noted that no negative velocities are evident.

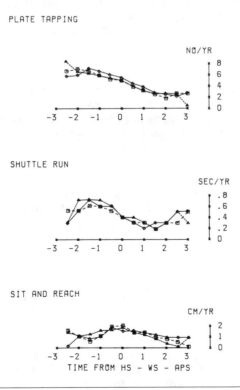

**Figure 32.** Age-at-spurt-based velocity curves for speed and flexibility measurements aligned on height spurt ( ▢——————▢ ), weight spurt ( ▢— – – —▢ ), and arm pull spurt ( ▲– – – ▲ ).

Flexibility (sit and reach, Figure 32)—Velocities on the HS-based curve increase from 0.1 cm/year 2.5 years before HS to 1.8 cm/year at 0.5 year before HS, and then slowly decrease to 0.9 cm/year at 3.0 years after HS. Velocities on the WS- and APS-based curves are more irregular before the spurts, but increase to about 2.0 cm/year just before and at WS and APS. They then decrease gradually to 0.0 cm/year 2.5 to 3.0 years after the spurts. If there is a spurt in this flexibility test, it seems to occur somewhat before HS, WS, or APS.

*Relationships Between Parameters of Different Measurements.* Interrelationships between the spurt and age at spurt are evaluated for the six variables for which the spurt and age at spurt could be calculated (see Data Analyses section). Means and standard deviations of the age at spurt and the growth spurt are given for these six variables in Table 10. The spurt in leg length occurs earliest and that in arm pull occurs latest. Between these extremes, the spurts in height, sitting height, weight, and chest circumference at inspiration occur during an interval of approximately 1 year. Standard deviations in the timing of the spurts vary between 1.2 years for the arm pull and 0.9 years for leg length. The magnitude of the spurt in leg length is similar to that in sitting height.

All means for the spurts reported in Table 10 are larger than the medians plotted on the graphs in the preceding section. This is due in part to the skewness of the distribution of velocities. For leg length, sitting height, and chest circumference, larger mean spurts can be expected, since the graphs of velocities of these measurements are plotted relative to HS or WS. In contrast, the maximum velocities shown in Table 10 are obtained at the time of the spurt in the measurement itself.

Correlations among the magnitude of the spurts in the six variables range from low to moderate (Table 11). The lowest correlations occur between the spurt in arm pull strength and the spurts in anthropometric dimensions. The highest correlations occur between the spurts of the length measurements, although the relationship between the spurts in leg length and sitting height is rather low.

**Table 10   Means and Standard Deviations of the Age at Spurt and Magnitude of Spurt in Several Anthropometric Dimensions and Static Strength**

|  | | Age at spurt (yrs) | | Spurt | |  |
|---|---|---|---|---|---|---|
|  | N | M | SD | M | SD |  |
| Leg length | 424 | 14.04 | 0.92 | 5.04 | 1.39 | cm/yr |
| Height | 432 | 14.22 | 0.97 | 9.21 | 1.61 | cm/yr |
| Sitting height | 427 | 14.33 | 0.99 | 5.32 | 1.19 | cm/yr |
| Weight | 429 | 14.56 | 1.16 | 8.77 | 2.33 | kg/yr |
| Chest circumference insp. | 428 | 14.70 | 1.10 | 6.80 | 1.68 | cm/yr |
| Arm pull | 413 | 15.00 | 1.23 | 17.56 | 4.83 | kg/yr |

**Table 11   Correlations Among Spurts
in Several Anthropometric Dimensions and Static Strength**

|  | Weight | Height | Sitting height | Leg length | Chest circumference | Arm pull |
|---|---|---|---|---|---|---|
| Weight | — | .30 | .21 | .18 | .40 | .29 |
|  |  | (425) | (420) | (417) | (427) | (342) |
| Height |  | — | .51 | .59 | .36 | .15 |
|  |  |  | (424) | (424) | (424) | (346) |
| Sitting height |  |  | — | .23 | .21 | .14 |
|  |  |  |  | (424) | (419) | (343) |
| Leg length |  |  |  | — | .22 | .10 |
|  |  |  |  |  | (416) | (341) |
| Chest circumference |  |  |  |  | — | .23 |
|  |  |  |  |  |  | (343) |

*Note.* For all correlations, $p < 0.01$, except $r = 0.10$, $p < 0.05$. The number of observations is indicated in parentheses.

Correlations among ages at the growth spurt in the different variables are higher, although the age at APS is only moderately correlated with the ages of the spurts in the anthropometric dimensions (Table 12). Finally, correlations between age at spurt and the magnitude of the spurt approach zero and are negative (Table 13).

**Table 12   Correlations Among Ages at Spurt
for Several Anthropometric Dimensions and Static Strength**

|  | Weight | Height | Sitting height | Leg length | Chest circumference | Arm pull |
|---|---|---|---|---|---|---|
| Weight | — | .68 | .55 | .50 | .50 | .32 |
|  |  | (425) | (420) | (417) | (421) | (342) |
| Height |  | — | .69 | .67 | .49 | .38 |
|  |  |  | (424) | (424) | (424) | (346) |
| Sitting height |  |  | — | .49 | .43 | .35 |
|  |  |  |  | (424) | (419) | (343) |
| Leg length |  |  |  | — | .37 | .23 |
|  |  |  |  |  | (416) | (341) |
| Chest circumference |  |  |  |  | — | .37 |
|  |  |  |  |  |  | (343) |

*Note.* For all correlations, $p < 0.01$. The number of observations is indicated in parentheses.

**Table 13   Correlations Between Magnitude of Spurt and Age
at Spurt in Each Anthropometric Dimension and Static Strength**

| Weight | Height | Sitting height | Leg length | Chest circumference | Arm pull |
|--------|--------|----------------|------------|---------------------|----------|
| −.01   | −.02   | −.06           | .05        | −.06                | .02      |
| (429)  | (432)  | (427)          | (424)      | (428)               | (413)    |

*Note.* None of the correlations are statistically significant. The number of observations is indicated in parentheses.

*Summary.*   The velocity curves of weight, lengths, circumferences, and trunk breadths are qualitatively similar to the height velocity curve. All show a reasonably defined increase immediately before, at, or immediately after the height spurt. The two extremity skeletal breadths show no clear increase in velocity, although a small spurt is apparent. The velocity curve of the triceps skinfold is U shaped and the velocities are negative from 1.0 year before HS. Calf skinfold velocities also decrease and become negative at HS. Velocities of the subscapular skinfold are positive and remain rather constant, while those for the suprailiac skinfold have an inverted U shape. They tend to become negative near the end of the age period under study.

The velocities of all motor items are positive throughout the age range considered. Static strength (arm pull), functional strength (bent arm hang), and explosive strength (vertical jump), and to a lesser extent flexibility (sit and reach), have a velocity curve that is similar in shape to the height velocity curve. The velocities for trunk strength fluctuate within a narrow range between 0 and 1 lift/sec, while the velocities for running speed (shuttle run) and speed of limb movement (plate tapping) gradually decrease, the decrease beginning well before HS.

A summary of the tentative timing of maximum velocities of all measurements relative to HS, WS, and APS is given in Table 14. Most maximum values of anthropometric dimensions are reached after HS, and before or coincident with WS. Only leg length, bicondylar breadth of the femur, thigh circumference, and calf circumference reach maximum velocities before HS. The three strength measurements attain maximum velocities after HS and WS, while speed and flexibility attain maximum velocities before HS and WS.

The synchronization of the height spurt is optimal when aligned on HS just as weight and arm pull strength are best aligned on their respective ages at spurt. The synchronization of the spurts in sitting height, leg length, biacromial and chest breadths, and the vertical jump is better when aligned on HS than when aligned on WS. Thigh and flexed arm circumferences are better synchronized on WS, while functional strength (bent arm hang) is better synchronized on APS. Both extremity skeletal breadths, chest and calf circumferences, and flexibility are similarly synchronized on HS and WS.

**Table 14  Timing of Maximum Observed Velocities of Anthropometric Dimensions and Motor Abilities Relative to Height Spurt, Weight Spurt, and Arm Pull Spurt**

| Measurement | Height spurt | | | Weight spurt | | | Arm pull spurt | | |
|---|---|---|---|---|---|---|---|---|---|
| | P[a] | C[b] | F[c] | P | C | F | P | C | F |
| Weight | | X | | X | | | X | | |
| Height | | X | | X | | | X | | |
| Sitting height | | X | | X | | | —[d] | — | — |
| Leg length | X | | | X | | | — | — | — |
| Biacromial breadth | | X | | | X | | — | — | — |
| Chest breadth | | X | | | X | | — | — | — |
| Biepicondylar breadth | | X | | X | | | — | — | — |
| Bicondylar breadth | X | | | X | | | — | — | — |
| Chest circumference | | X | | X | | | — | — | — |
| Flexed arm circumference | | X | | | X | | X | | |
| Thigh circumference | X | | | | X | | — | — | — |
| Calf circumference | X | | | X | | | — | — | — |
| Arm pull | | X | | | | X | | | X |
| Vertical jump | | X | | | | X | | | X |
| Bent arm hang | | X | | | | X | | | X |
| Plate tapping | X | | | | X | | X | | |
| Shuttle run | X | | | | X | | X | | |
| Sit and reach | X | | | | X | | X | | |

[a]Spurt of measurement precedes HS, WS, or APS; [b]coincides with HS, WS, or APS; [c]follows HS, WS, or APS. [d]Measurements not considered relative to APS.

## Discussion

Although physical performance is an important factor in the behavioral repertoire of children and youth, serial data on motor performance are generally lacking or inadequately analyzed. Most of our present knowledge on the timing and sequence of motor performance relative to somatic growth during adolescence is restricted largely to muscular strength in several longitudinal studies (Carron & Bailey, 1974; Ellis et al., 1975; Espenschade, 1940; Faust, 1977; Jones, 1949; Stolz & Stolz, 1951). The Leuven Growth Study considers a broader spectrum of the gross motor domain and relates the developmental patterns in motor items to growth in a variety of bodily dimensions including mass, lengths, skeletal breadths, trunk and limb circumferences, and subcutaneous fat in a large longitudinal sample of boys.

The design of the study inevitably has several limitations; for example, observations were made only at yearly intervals and not at exact birth dates, and only boys in the age range 12 to 20 years were included. These limitations in turn have consequences for the analyses of the serial data available. First, most of the existing mathematical models for fitting or smoothing growth data could not be applied since only six measurements were available. Second, age at peak velocity and peak velocity could not be well defined in contrast to studies in which children were measured at 6-month or even 3-month intervals. And third, early maturing boys, who ordinarily show a peak velocity in the commonly used growth measurements at or before the age of first examination in the Leuven study, that is, 11.75 to 13.25 years, were excluded from the analysis for the definition of the spurt and age at spurt.

In order to overcome these limitations, methods of analysis designed to make maximal use of the available data were developed. Six-month velocities were calculated using polynomials without smoothing. The spurt and age at spurt were calculated for only those variables that met a series of six selection criteria. In addition, three types of curves were constructed: chronological age-based distance curves, age-based velocity curves, and age-at-spurt-based velocity curves. For the age-at-spurt-based curves, growth and performance data were aligned only on the ages at height spurt, weight spurt, and arm pull spurt. These three measurements met the criteria that were established to define an age at spurt and the spurt itself. Further, height and weight are the two commonly used anthropometric dimensions, while the arm pull is the best performance variable by the established criteria.

Before distance and velocity curves were presented, the representativeness of the longitudinal sample was considered by comparing the sample to Belgian reference data. Identical measuring and testing procedures were used in constructing the reference data, since the longitudinal and cross-sectional data were gathered during the same study and at the same measuring periods. At the younger ages considered, median values of the longitudinal sample consistently fall below those of the reference group. The lowest medians are situated at the P 34 value, which corresponds to a value of the mean minus one standard deviation. At the older ages, the medians of the longitudinal sample correspond to those of the reference data. These two trends imply that the longitudinal sample consisted largely of average and late maturing boys, and that due to the selection procedures used in the longitudinal analysis, the most early maturing boys were excluded. Thus, the median curves presented for the longitudinal series should not be used as reference data for the Belgian population.

The preceding is a reasonable assumption. Estimated mean ages at spurt for height and weight in the Leuven series are quite similar to estimated ages at peak height and weight velocity in Swedish boys classified as average maturing (Lindgren, 1978). For example, estimated ages at peak height velocity in Belgian boys and average maturing Swedish boys are identical, at 14.2 years. In contrast, the mean age at peak height velocity for early maturing Swedish boys is 12.5 years, and the mean age at peak height velocity for the total Swedish sample is 14.1 years. Similarly for body weight, mean age at spurt in Belgian boys is 14.6 years, while age at peak weight velocity for average maturing Swedish boys is 14.4 years.

In contrast, the mean age at peak weight velocity in early maturing Swedish boys is 13.1 years, and that for the total sample is 14.3 years. Hence, it is reasonable to assume that the Belgian sample excludes most early maturing boys, and as such, median curves for the longitudinal series should not be used as reference values for the Belgian population. Distance curves derived from the total sample, that is, the longitudinal and cross-sectional components (Ostyn et al., 1980), are more appropriate as reference data. The data include larger samples and a broader cross-section of the maturity spectrum, particularly at the younger ages of the range considered in the Leuven study.

## Chronological Age-Based Distance and Velocity Curves

Since Buffon and his collaborators measured fetuses and children in the 1740s (Tanner, 1981), numerous descriptions of the growth curves of stature and several anthropometric dimensions have been given. The chronological age-based distance curves of most anthropometric dimensions considered in this study show the S-shaped form so often described for growth in the adolescent period. All anthropometric dimensions, with the exception of skinfolds, increase considerably during the adolescent period, following the S-shaped pattern of initial slow growth, a rapid increase in growth, and then a gradual tapering. Weight, lengths, and trunk breadths and circumferences show a maximum velocity between 14.0 and 15.0 years. A plateau rather than a sharp peak is apparent for weight and the flexed arm and calf circumferences. This result could be due to the so-called time-spreading effect described by Tanner (1951, 1962). Since children tend to grow at different rates, there is considerable variation in the time taken to reach developmental milestones such as peak velocity. For the extremity bone breadths (biepicondylar humerus and bicondylar femur), no real peak or plateau is apparent in the velocity curves.

Distance and velocity curves of the four skinfolds differ considerably from other body measurements. The two skinfolds measured on the trunk gradually increase in thickness linearly with age through adolescence. Velocities of the subscapular and suprailiac skinfolds are rather constant prior to 14 years of age, after which they decline slightly. After 16 years of age, however, velocities of the two trunk skinfolds differ markedly. They increase slightly to early adolescent levels for the subscapular skinfold, but decline considerably for the suprailiac skinfold.

Skinfolds measured on the extremities, in contrast to those on the trunk, show a different pattern. Both increase early in adolescence and then decline in thickness at the time of the growth spurt. Velocities of the triceps skinfold become negative after 14.5 years of age, while those for the calf skinfold become negative at about 15 years of age.

The different distance and velocity patterns for trunk and extremity skinfold thicknesses thus suggest a change in the distribution of subcutaneous fat during male adolescence. Of particular interest may be the difference between the upper trunk (subscapular) and lower trunk (suprailiac) sites after the height spurt. Current interest in the significance of variation in fat distribution or fat patterning for a variety of metabolic measurements, some of which are risk factors for cardiovascular disease and diabetes (Bjorntorp, 1985; Stern & Haffner, 1986), emphasizes the need to consider individual variation in fat distribution longitudinally during adolescence.

The differences in development of skinfold thicknesses on the trunk and on the extremities during adolescence are consistent with other data (Johnston, Hamill, & Lemeshow, 1974; Tanner & Whitehouse, 1975). The evidence also suggests that the decrease in thickness of the subcutaneous fat layer of the extremities is not due to growth of the underlying muscle and bone; rather, it appears to be an actual loss of subcutaneous fat on the extremities close to the time of the adolescent growth spurt.

Chronological age-based medians for highest velocity, age at highest velocity, and attained size at highest velocity for anthropometric dimensions are summarized in Table 15. The term highest velocity was chosen since this value does not consistently correspond to the peak value obtained by aligning the velocity curves on the age at peak. Median peak velocities derived from data aligned on age at spurt are consistently higher than the highest velocities based on chrono-

**Table 15   Median Highest Velocity, Age at Highest Velocity, and Attained Size at Highest Velocity Based on Chronological Age for Anthropometric Dimensions**

|  | N | Highest velocity | Age (years) at highest velocity | Attained size at highest velocity |
|---|---|---|---|---|
| Weight | 274 | 6.2 kg/yr (7.9 kg/yr) | 14.5 | 48.5 kg |
| Height | 276 | 8.0 cm/yr (8.9 cm/yr) | 14.5 | 160.9 cm |
| Sitting height | 271 | 4.0 cm/yr (4.4 cm/yr) | 14.5 | 82.7 cm |
| Leg length | 271 | 3.8 cm/yr (4.3 cm/yr) | 14.5 | 76.3 cm |
| Biacromial breadth | 274 | 2.2 cm/yr (2.3 cm/yr) | 15.0 | 36.0 cm |
| Chest breadth | 272 | 1.9 cm/yr (1.7 cm/yr) | 15.0 | 26.2 cm |
| Biepicondylar breadth | 265 | 3.9 mm/yr (3.1 mm/yr) | 15.0 | 6.9 cm |
| Bicondylar breadth | 267 | 2.8 mm/yr (3.0 mm/yr) | 14.75 | 9.4 cm |
| Chest circumference inspiration | 270 | 4.7 cm/yr (5.2 cm/yr) | 14.75 | 83.2 cm |
| Flexed arm circumference | 271 | 1.5 cm/yr (2.0 cm/yr) | 14.75 | 24.2 cm |

*Note.* Values in parentheses are median maximal velocities derived from the data aligned on age at spurt in height or weight, whichever yielded the maximum value.

logical age, with the exception of chest and biepicondylar breadths. These observations emphasize the need to appropriately analyze and synchronize longitudinal data on biological milestones for the evaluation of growth velocities during adolescence. This was initially suggested by Boas (1892), first applied by Shuttleworth (1937), theoretically based and explained by Tanner (1951), and eventually made available by Tanner et al. (1966) for assessing the acceleration or deceleration of growth in the height and weight of an individual.

The present analysis also illustrates that the alignment of growth velocities on the height or weight spurt influences considerably the magnitude of the estimated velocities. This observation has practical implications for the construction of velocity reference data for different body dimensions. In aligning velocities on an accurately defined age-at-height spurt, or age-at-weight spurt, the time-spreading effect is significantly reduced. Moreover, it should also be noted that the age at peak velocity for some measurements cannot be precisely defined, since the measurement error is of the same magnitude as the observed increments during short intervals (see Van't Hof, Beunen, & Simons, n.d.). Hence, the alignment of body measurements on age at spurt in height or weight may have value for the construction of velocity standards for such measurements.

It is well established that the motor performance of boys increases considerably during adolescence (Clarke, 1971; Espenschade, 1940, 1960; Jones, 1949; Malina, 1974, 1980). The motor tests used in this study include a variety of gross motor performances and measure mutually independent factors (Simons et al., 1969). A significant improvement in performance occurs in all tests. The performance-attained curves of static strength (arm pull), explosive strength (vertical jump), functional strength (bent arm hang), speed of limb movement (plate tapping), and running speed (shuttle run) show the S-shaped pattern previously described for a number of anthropometric characteristics. Flexibility (sit and reach) shows a less clear S-shaped curve, while trunk strength (leg lifts) shows only a slight improvement over adolescence.

The increase in muscular strength during adolescence is more than expected from the increase in body size (Asmussen, 1973; Asmussen & Heebøll-Nielson, 1955, 1956; Carron & Bailey, 1974), assuming a proportional increase in all body dimensions. This increase may perhaps be related to the doubling of the estimated number of muscle nuclei in males from 9 through 14 years of age (Cheek, 1968). The disproportionate strength increase in male adolescence is more apparent in strength of the upper extremities than in strength of the trunk or lower extremities (Malina, 1986a). Since the muscle mass of the arm doubles during male adolescence (Baker et al., 1958; Malina, 1986a; Malina & Johnston, 1967), it may be plausible to hypothesize a relationship between body composition and strength increments. Indeed, arm pull strength and the bent arm hang are measures that involve primarily the upper arm musculature.

The rather small increase in trunk strength may be related to the significant increase in length and mass of the lower extremities, in contrast to a lesser increase in the pelvic and abdominal musculature that is stressed in the leg lift test. The smaller increase in trunk strength may also be a function of the test procedures. The subject had to raise and lower the legs as quickly as possible during 20 seconds. Due to the time limit, maximal performance is also limited. The P 95 values for the Belgian reference population vary between 19 and 20 lifts per

20 seconds from 12 through 20 years, whereas the lowest performance, that is, no lifts, is also the same for each age group (Ostyn et al., 1980).

Thus the strength increase in the muscles of the pelvic and abdominal regions relative to body size is less than the relative strength increase in the upper extremity and upper trunk region. The apparent regional differences in strength development are perhaps related to the growth of the musculature in different parts of the body, and some observations suggest variation in muscle mass increments in different body regions (Malina, 1986a).

The three components of muscular strength, static, functional, and explosive, show a velocity curve qualitatively similar to that for body size and several dimensions, and have a clear maximum velocity at 15.0 or 15.5 years. The velocities for the fourth strength component (trunk strength) vary between 0 and 1 lift/year. The velocities for flexibility also remain fairly stable, varying between 1 and 2 cm/year. For the two speed factors, speed of limb movement (plate tapping) and running speed (shuttle run), velocities are maximal at 13 to 14 years of age and gradually decrease over adolescence. However, they do not reach zero or become negative.

Medians of the age at highest velocity, highest velocity itself, and attained performance at highest velocity are summarized in Table 16 for the motor perfor-

**Table 16   Median Highest Velocity, Age at Highest Velocity, and Attained Performance at Highest Velocity Based on Chronological Age for Motor Performance Items**

|  | N | Highest velocity | Age (years) at highest velocity | Attained performance at highest velocity |
|---|---|---|---|---|
| Arm pull | 219 | 11.9 kg/yr (15.0 kg/yr) | 15.0 | 50.0 kg |
| Vertical jump | 222 | 4.5 cm/yr (4.8 cm/yr) | 15.0 | 39.0 cm |
| Bent arm hang | 217 | 5.5 sec/yr (5.1 sec/yr) | 15.5 | 26.5 sec |
| Leg lifts[a] | 213 | 1 lift/yr (1 lift/yr) | 15.25 | 15.5 # |
| Plate tapping[b] | 213 | 7 taps/yr (8.2 taps/yr) | 14.0 | 83.0 # |
| Shuttle run[b] | 210 | 0.7 sec/yr (0.7 sec/yr) | 13.5 | 22.3 sec |
| Sit and reach[a] | 218 | 1.5 cm/yr (2.0 cm/yr) | 15.5 | 22.0 cm |

*Note.* Values in parentheses are maximal velocities derived from the data aligned on age at spurt in height, weight, or arm pull, whichever yielded the maximum value.

[a]Highest velocity not clearly defined; [b]Highest velocity occurs at beginning of observation period and is not necessarily the spurt or peak value.

mance items. As noted earlier, the highest velocities for the two speed tests occur at the beginning of the age period under consideration, and should not be interpreted as the spurt or as peak values since data on the performance at earlier age levels are not available. However, the evidence suggests that a peak occurs at an early age. It is difficult to define an age at highest velocity for trunk strength and flexibility since there is little variation in the observed velocities. The age at highest velocity in the three strength components for which a clear peak in velocity was observed is 15.0 or 15.5 years. For static strength (arm pull), the alignment of the velocities on a biological parameter has a considerable effect on the magnitude of the spurt. The same is true to a lesser extent for explosive strength (vertical jump), while alignment on the height, weight, or arm pull spurts has little effect on the magnitude of the spurt in functional strength (bent arm hang). It is not certain whether the maximum value would be larger if the velocities were aligned on the age at spurt in bent arm hang performance.

## Age-at-Spurt-Based Distance and Velocity Curves

Before discussing the velocities of measurements aligned on HS, WS, or APS, the age at spurt and magnitude of the spurt for selected measurements are compared with those reported in the literature. Mean ages at peak velocity and peak velocity for height obtained in several studies of European and North American boys are summarized in Tables 17 and 18, respectively. Results obtained with the double logistic model (e.g., Thissen, Bock, Wainer, & Roche, 1976) tend

**Table 17  Estimated Ages at Peak Height Velocity (Years) in Several Studies of European and North American Boys**

| Study | Reference | Method | N | M | SD |
|---|---|---|---|---|---|
| Berkeley | Nicolson & Hanley (1953) | Graphical | 86 | 13.8 | 1.2 |
| Berkeley | Bock & Thissen (1980) | Triple logistic | 66 | 13.7 | 1.1 |
| Denver | Deming (1957) | Gompertz | 24 | 13.4 | 0.9 |
| Denver | Hansman & Maresh (1961) | Graphical | 27 | 14.0 | 1.0 |
| Harpenden | Tanner et al. (1966) | Graphical | 49 | 14.1 | 0.9 |
| Harpenden | Tanner et al. (1976) | Single logistic | 55 | 13.9 | 0.8 |
| Harpenden | Preece & Baines (1978) | Preece-Baines I | 35 | 14.2 | 0.9 |
| Newcastle | Billewicz et al. (1981) | Graphical | 653 | 14.1 | 1.0 |
| Paris | Roy (1972) | Graphical | 68 | 13.8 | 0.9 |
| Zurich | Largo et al. (1976) | Splines | 112 | 13.9 | 0.8 |
| Stockholm | Taranger et al. (1976) | Moving increments | 122 | 14.1 | 1.1 |
| Sweden, urban | Lindgren (1978) | Midyear velocity | 373 | 14.1 | 1.1 |
| Wrocław | Bielicki et al. (1984) | Graphical | 177 | 14.0 | 1.2 |
| Saskatchewan | Mirwald & Bailey (1986) | Preece-Baines I | 75 | 14.3 | 1.0 |
| Leiden | Wafelbakker (1969) | ? | 81 | 14.4 | — |
| Amsterdam | Kemper et al. (1985) | 2nd-degree polynomials | 120 | 14.0 | — |
| Leuven | Present study | Nonsmoothed polynomials | 432 | 14.2 | 1.0 |

**Table 18    Estimated Peak Height Velocity (cm/year)
in Several Studies of European and North American Boys**

| Study | Reference | Method | N | M | SD |
|-------|-----------|--------|---|---|----|
| Harpenden | Tanner et al. (1966) | Graphical | 49 | 10.3 | 1.5 |
| Harpenden | Tanner et al. (1976) | Single logistic | 55 | 8.8 | 1.1 |
| Harpenden | Preece & Baines (1978) | Preece-Baines I | 35 | 8.2 | 1.2 |
| Newcastle | Billewicz et al. (1981) | Graphical | 539 | 9.6 | 1.2 |
| Paris | Roy (1972) | Graphical | 68 | 9.7 | 1.1 |
| Zurich | Largo et al. (1978) | Splines | 112 | 9.0 | 1.1 |
| Stockholm | Taranger et al. (1976) | Moving increments | 122 | 9.9 | 1.1 |
| Sweden, urban | Lindgren (1978) | Midyear velocity | 354 | 9.8 | 1.4 |
| Saskatchewan | Mirwald & Bailey (1986) | Preece-Baines I | 75 | 9.4 | 1.5 |
| Amsterdam | Kemper et al. (1985) | 2nd-degree polynomials | 96 | 9.6 | — |
| Leuven | Present study | Nonsmoothed polynomials | 432 | 9.2 | 1.6 |

to consistently underestimate age at peak height velocity and peak velocity compared to other models and methods (Hauspie et al., 1980), and thus are not included. Nevertheless, there is variation among methods used to estimate age at peak height velocity and peak velocity. Mean ages at peak height velocity among boys in the different samples are reasonably similar, with the exception of Deming's (1957) estimate of 13.4 years, based on a Gompertz curve, for a small sample of boys from the Child Research Council in Denver. The graphic estimate for 27 boys from the Child Research Council is 14.0 years, however, and is similar to estimates from the other studies. With the exception of Deming's (1957) low estimate, all other estimated mean ages at peak height velocity range between 13.7 and 14.4 years.

The mean age at spurt for height in Belgian boys is at the upper end of the range of means in Table 17 and may reflect the exclusion of very early maturing boys from the sample. Standard deviations for estimated ages at peak height velocity vary between 0.8 and 1.2 years, and that for Belgian boys falls within this range.

The peak velocity observed in the Leuven series lies well within the range given in other studies (8.2 to 10.3 cm/year). The 10.3 cm/year obtained in the graphical analysis by Tanner et al. (1966) probably overestimates somewhat the value at peak. At the time of graphical fitting, Tanner and colleagues believed the spurt to be fairly sharply peaked (Marubini et al., 1972). The standard deviation of 1.5 cm/year is also larger than in other studies, and is probably due to the mathematical model used. The model does not force a preliminary set shape through the observed points.

Mean ages at peak velocity and peak velocities for several anthropometric dimensions and static strength are given in Table 19. Sitting height in the Wrocław study was measured as trunk length (sitting height of cervicale), while leg length was measured as symphysion height. Nevertheless, there is a close correspondence among the Harpenden, Wrocław, and Leuven data for the age at peak (spurt) in sitting height, while the age at peak (spurt) in leg length is 0.4 year later in the Leuven series. Since the spurt in leg length occurs earlier than that in sitting height, the omission of very early maturers in the Leuven sample probably influences the results.

The age at spurt in body weight of urban Swedish and Wrocław boys is, on average, 0.3 year earlier than in Leuven boys. This difference may reflect the different techniques of estimating the ages at peak velocity, and perhaps the

**Table 19    Mean Ages at Peak Velocity and Peak Velocities for Several Anthropometric Dimensions and Static Strength in Longitudinal Studies**

| Dimension | Study | References | Method | N | M | SD |
|---|---|---|---|---|---|---|
| *Age at Peak Velocity (years)* | | | | | | |
| Height | Harpenden | Tanner et al. (1976) | Logistic | 55 | 13.9 | 0.8 |
| | Wrocław | Bielicki et al. (1984) | Graphical | 177 | 14.0 | 1.2 |
| | Leuven | Present study | Polynomial | 432 | 14.2 | 1.0 |
| Sitting height | Harpenden | Tanner et al. (1976) | Logistic | 55 | 14.3 | 0.9 |
| | Wrocław | Bielicki et al. (1984) | Graphical | 177 | 14.4 | 1.1 |
| | Leuven | Present study | Polynomial | 427 | 14.3 | 1.0 |
| Leg length | Harpenden | Tanner et al. (1976) | Logistic | 55 | 13.6 | 0.8 |
| | Wrocław | Bielicki et al. (1984) | Graphical | 177 | 13.6 | 1.1 |
| | Leuven | Present study | Polynomial | 424 | 14.0 | 0.9 |
| Weight | Sweden, urban | Lindgren (1978) | Midyear | 339 | 14.3 | 1.1 |
| | Wrocław | Bielicki et al. (1984) | Graphical | 177 | 14.3 | 1.2 |
| | Leuven | Present study | Polynomial | 429 | 14.6 | 1.2 |
| Static strength | California[a] | Stolz & Stolz (1951) | Graphical | 66 | 1 yr after PHV | |
| | Saskatchewan[b] | Carron & Bailey (1974) | Graphical | 99 | 1 yr after PHV | |
| | Leuven | Present study | Polynomial | 413 | 15.0 | 1.2 |
| *Peak Velocity* | | | | | | |
| Height | Harpenden | Tanner et al. (1976) | Logistic | 55 | 8.8 | 1.1 |
| (cm/yr) | Leuven | Present study | Polynomial | 432 | 9.2 | 1.6 |
| Sitting height | Harpenden | Tanner et al. (1976) | Logistic | 55 | 4.5 | 0.7 |
| (cm/yr) | Leuven | Present study | Polynomial | 427 | 5.3 | 1.2 |
| Leg length | Harpenden | Tanner et al. (1976) | Logistic | 55 | 4.3 | 0.7 |
| (cm/yr) | Leuven | Present study | Polynomial | 424 | 5.0 | 1.4 |
| Weight | Sweden, urban | Lindgren (1978) | Midyear | 339 | 9.1 | 2.0 |
| (kg/yr) | Leuven | Present study | Polynomial | 429 | 8.8 | 2.3 |

[a]Stolz and Stolz (1951) used the sum of scores for left and right handgrip, shoulder pull, and shoulder thrust; [b]Carron and Bailey (1974) used upper body, lower body, and total strength composite scores from nine isometric strength tests.

exclusion of very early maturing boys in the Leuven sample. The general observations of Stolz and Stolz (1951) and Carron and Bailey (1974) on muscular strength are consistent with the Leuven data. The strength spurt occurs about 0.8 year after the height spurt in Leuven boys.

The mean velocities and standard deviations for Leuven boys (see Table 19) are larger than those reported by Tanner et al. (1976). The differences might reflect the mathematical model used. Measurements in the Harpenden study were obtained at 3-month intervals, while those in the Leuven study were taken at yearly intervals, although the velocities were estimated for half-year intervals. Tanner et al. (1976) also showed that when annual rather than quarterly measurements are used, the maximum yearly velocities for height are lowered from 9.8 to 8.9 cm/year. Taking into account the elimination of very early maturing boys in the Leuven study, the velocity of 9.2 cm/year is probably a good estimate of the maximum velocity. Further, the single logistic model slightly underestimates the true velocities (Tanner et al., 1976).

The correlations between age at spurt and the spurt in selected anthropometric dimensions and static strength of Leuven boys approximate zero, but are negative (see Table 13). Although Tanner et al. (1976) and Lindgren (1978) observed rather low correlations between age at peak and peak velocity of height, sitting height, and weight, respectively, Lindgren suggested that the lower correlations might be an effect of the methods used in defining the age at peak. Correlations between the spurts in length measurements in Leuven boys (0.23 to 0.59, see Table 11) are of the same magnitude as those reported for the Harpenden data (0.17 to 0.72, Tanner et al., 1976). Correlations between the ages at spurt in length measurements in the Leuven study (0.49 to 0.69, see Table 12), however, are considerably lower than those of Harpenden (0.93 to 0.97, Tanner et al., 1976) and Wrocław boys (0.89 to 0.95, Bielicki, Koniarek, & Malina, 1984). The less precise definition of the age at spurt may influence the correlations in Leuven boys.

The velocities of weight, lengths, circumferences, and trunk breadths have a similar shape as the height velocity curve. Limb bone breadths have only a small spurt. The velocities of the extremity skinfolds are negative before or at the HS, while subscapular skinfold velocities remain stable and suprailiac skinfold velocities show a small peak. Most anthropometric dimensions reach a maximum velocity after HS, and before or coincident with WS. Only leg length, bicondylar breadth of the femur, and thigh and calf circumferences reach a maximum velocity in the half-year interval preceding the height spurt.

The data of Tanner and colleagues (Marubini et al., 1972; Tanner et al., 1976) based on fitted single logistic curves for Harpenden children indicate that peak velocity in leg length precedes peak height velocity, while the velocities for sitting height, biacromial breadth, and bicristal breadth occur at or after the peak height velocity. The earlier spurt in leg length relative to height is well established (Malina, 1978). Roche (1974), for example, considered the timing of growth in the lengths of individual long bones of the extremities. Peak velocity in tibial length preceded peak height velocity, while peak velocity in radius length occurred at or after peak height velocity.

Tanner et al. (1981) analyzed radiographically determined widths of bone, muscle, and fat in the upper arm and calf relative to peak velocities and the timing of peak velocities in several anthropometric dimensions. Muscle widths attain peak velocity more coincident with peak sitting height velocity than with peak height velocity. The peak velocities of tibial and humeral widths coincide with peak height velocity. Fat widths of the arm show a nadir that coincides with peak height velocity, while those of the calf show a nadir 6 months after peak height velocity. Thus it appears that muscle widths, circumferences, and trunk breadths have their maximum velocity within 6 months after peak height velocity and more coincident with the weight spurt. The earlier occurrence of the maximum velocity in thigh and calf circumferences relative to the height spurt in the Leuven series might be explained by the inclusion of subcutaneous tissue in the measurements.

Extremity skinfolds tend to decrease during the height spurt, thus reducing the velocities of limb circumferences. However, the maximum increase in the muscle of the upper arm is relatively larger (10 mm/year) than the maximum velocity of the calf (8 mm/year, Tanner et al., 1981). Apparently, the relatively greater spurt in muscle tissue of the arm offsets the reduction in subcutaneous fat on the arm so that arm circumference is probably not markedly affected by the decrease in arm fat. The negative velocities in limb skinfolds at the triceps and calf sites at HS correspond closely with the observations of Tanner et al. (1981) for radiographically determined arm and calf fat and are very similar to the pseudovelocity curve for the triceps skinfold reported by Johnston et al. (1974).

The variability of ages at spurt for body dimensions and static strength is similar to that for stature. Interindividual variability in the timing of a specific dimension is larger than the variability in timing of mean ages at spurt, which spans about 1 year (14.0 years for leg length and 15.0 years for static strength). Roche (1974) observed similar interindividual variability in bone lengths of the extremities, resulting in sequence variability within subjects. Roche noted that if, as is generally accepted, adolescent changes result from a single trigger mechanism in the central nervous system, and that the adolescent changes reflect responses to altered levels of circulating hormones, this trigger mechanism "is part of an inaccurate widebore shotgun" (p. 156).

The synchronization of the spurts in sitting height, leg length, and biacromial and chest breadths is better when aligned on HS than when aligned on WS. For thigh and flexed arm circumferences the synchronization is better on WS than on HS. For all other anthropometric dimensions included in this study, no differences in the magnitude of the spurt are observed when the velocities are aligned on HS or WS. It is not surprising that bone lengths and diameters are better synchronized on HS, while flexed arm and thigh circumferences are better synchronized on WS. The spurt in height is really a composite of lower extremity bone lengths and trunk dimensions. The spurt in weight, on the other hand, is a composite of all body tissues, including especially muscle and skeletal mass. Limb circumferences are comprised largely of muscle tissue. Hence, it comes as no surprise that the spurts in thigh and flexed arm circumferences are better synchronized with the spurt for body weight.

Median velocities of all motor items are positive during the age range studied. There is no evidence that the period of rapid growth during adolescence, that is, the height spurt, is a period of so-called "adolescent awkwardness" or the "overgrown, clumsy" age (Tanner, 1962; Ungerer, 1973) commonly reported in developmental and physical education textbooks. All motor items increase significantly during male adolescence and have a growth spurt just before, at, or just after HS, with the exception of speed of movement and trunk strength.

The maximum velocities in running speed and speed of limb movement, however, presumably occur before the HS. Well defined spurts in three strength tests—static strength (arm pull), explosive strength (vertical jump), and functional strength (bent arm hang)—are apparent in the Leuven data and the velocity curves are similar to that for height. All three strength tasks show a spurt after the spurts in height and weight, and coincident with the spurt in static strength (arm pull). The late occurrence of the spurt in static strength is consistent with the findings of Stolz and Stolz (1951) and of Carron and Bailey (1974). In both studies, the apex in strength occurred approximately 1 year after the height spurt.

On the other hand, the Leuven results for explosive and functional strength are clearly different from those of the Saskatchewan Growth Study (Ellis et al., 1975). For the flexed arm hang (functional strength) and standing broad jump (explosive strength), the maximum velocities occurred during the period of peak height velocity in the Saskatchewan study. In the Leuven study, the spurts in functional strength (bent arm hang, same test as the Saskatchewan Growth Study) and explosive strength (vertical jump) occurred nearly 1 year after the height spurt. It is not clear whether this apparent difference in timing is due to the differences in techniques used to define the age at peak velocity and the velocities in the different tests. The procedures used in the Saskatchewan study start with the raw increments without any other modification and lead to an imprecise definition of maximum velocities.

The age range in the Saskatchewan Growth Study, 10 to 16 years, also contributes to the differences. The Saskatchewan study most likely includes more early maturing and fewer later maturing boys than the Leuven study, for which the converse is the case. What is puzzling, however, is the observation in the Saskatchewan study of a spurt in static strength 1 year after height velocity (Carron & Bailey, 1974), while the spurts in functional and explosive strength occur coincidently with peak height velocity (Ellis et al., 1975).

The lack of a clear spurt in trunk strength (leg lifts) of Leuven boys may be related to the test itself. The time limit of the test sets a limit on the maximal performance, and maximal performances are attained in early adolescence. Other possible contributing factors are the earlier spurt in leg length and the relatively lesser increase in lower extremity compared to upper extremity strength (Carron & Bailey, 1974).

The velocities for flexibility (sit and reach) vary between 1 and 2 cm/year, and it is difficult to detect a spurt. It should be noted, however, that even for this test no decrease in performance is seen. Although estimated increments from the cross-sectional study of Merni, Balboni, Bargellini, and Menegatti (1981) demonstrated a loss in flexibility in several joints over age, trunk forward flexion showed no apparent decrease between 12 and 17 years. These results are probably explained in part by the increase in strength of the abdominal muscles during adolescence. These muscles in turn influence trunk forward flexion to some extent. Correlations between sit and reach and trunk strength (leg lifts), for example, vary between .29 and .42 in Belgian boys (Simons et al., 1969).

The alignment of the velocities in explosive strength (vertical jump) on HS results in a somewhat higher maximum than when aligned on WS or APS. The alignment of the velocities in functional strength (bent arm hang) on APS results in the highest maximum. This implies that for explosive strength the time-spreading effect is more reduced when aligned on HS than when aligned on the WS or APS spurts, indicating a better association between HS and vertical jump spurt.

# Implications

Implications of studies of growth and performance are many, and only some are considered here. Adolescence is characteristically variable in timing, intensity, and duration among individuals. In order to control for the different chronological ages at which the adolescent spurt occurs in individual children, the events of adolescence are commonly viewed relative to the timing of the adolescent spurt in height, that is, the age at peak height velocity. Hence, growth in other body dimensions and tissues can be expressed in terms of time before and after the height spurt. This procedure has been applied largely to anthropometric and body composition variables, but only to a limited extent to motor performance tasks. Results of the Leuven study thus add to the rich literature on male adolescence by reporting adolescent spurts in several motor performance items and expressing them relative to the traditional marker of the adolescent spurt in longitudinal studies, age at peak height velocity.

Age at peak height velocity and peak height velocity itself have high heritabilities (Fischbein, 1977; Skład, 1977). Age at peak height velocity is also highly correlated with indices of sexual and skeletal maturation during adolescence, both of which also have a high heritability. Hence, under adequate environmental circumstances, the adolescent growth spurt and sexual maturation are to a large extent genetically determined; that is, they are individual characteristics.

Corresponding data on the heritability of adolescent spurts in motor performance variables are not available. Muscular strength is highly correlated with male sexual maturation, however, so it is reasonable to assume that the adolescent spurt in muscular strength is also a highly individual characteristic. Indeed, the three strength tests used in the present study show adolescent spurts following those for height and more coincident with the spurt for body weight. Studies of twins suggest a significant genotypic component of the variance in a number of strength tests. However, the estimates are lower than those for stature and the majority fall in the moderate range. Estimates of heritability for strength tests also vary among studies, tasks, and types of genetically related individuals considered, that is, twins, siblings, parents and offspring, and so on (see Bouchard & Malina, 1983; Malina, 1986b). Further, studies of the genetics of muscular strength do not include estimates of the genotypic component of variance in the strength spurt that occurs during male adolescence.

The evidence for adolescent spurts in two speed tests and flexibility is not clear. Data from this longitudinal series of Belgian boys suggest that if spurts in these performance tasks occur, they probably occur prior to the adolescent spurt in height. Estimates of the genotypic component of variance in tests of speed and flexibility are reasonably similar to those for muscular strength (Bouchard & Malina, 1983; Malina, 1986b).

In light of these observations on motor performance and specifically muscular strength, the popular notion of a boy "outgrowing his strength" during the adolescent spurt (e.g., see Tanner, 1962, 1978) does not find support in this longitudinal analysis. During puberty there is no period when strength ceases to increase, irrespective of its different components. Rather, strength increases markedly even during the height spurt. At HS, static strength (arm pull) increases by 11.7 kg/year, and none of the 219 boys followed longitudinally has a negative velocity during this period. The estimated velocity at HS is 30% of attained static strength at this time. Similarly, the estimated velocities of functional strength (bent arm hang) and explosive strength (vertical jump) at HS are only slightly lower than at their respective maximal values. When expressed as a percentage of attained strength at HS, the velocities are, respectively, 25% and 12%. In contrast, the velocity of statural growth at HS is 5.5% of attained height at this time. Even for trunk strength, velocity at HS is approximately 7% of attained strength at this time. Although the apex in strength development occurs after HS, strength velocities at HS are considerable, and there is no reason to accept the notion of a boy's outgrowing his strength during this period of rapid growth.

Along the same lines, median velocities for all motor items are positive during adolescence. Thus there is no indication in this longitudinal study of a period of adolescent awkwardness or of an overgrown, clumsy age, concepts that were common in the earlier developmental literature. However, Tanner (1978) indicates a possible period during the growth spurt, lasting no more than 6 months, when there may be temporary problems with balance that affect performance in certain tasks. Tanner relates the period to the time when trunk length has increased relative to length of the legs prior to the attainment of full size and strength of the muscles. No balance task was included in the Leuven study, but evidence from the various strength tests, as noted above, does not indicate any temporary slowdown in the development of static, functional, or explosive strength during the growth spurt. On the other hand, annual observations may not be sufficiently sensitive to detect a period of incoordination, if such a period exists at all.

The changes in size and motor performance during the adolescent spurt have a significant impact on proficiency in sports skills. The influence of variation in maturity status on the physical performance of boys, however, has typically been examined in comparisons of boys of the same chronological age. Thus, within a given chronological age group, boys classified as advanced in maturity status generally perform better than boys classified as average or late in maturity status. The differences among boys in contrasting maturity groups are, in part, a function of the size and strength advantage of the early maturing boys. As late maturing boys begin to catch up in size and strength, the disadvantage they faced previously in physical performance may be considerably reduced.

Thus the adolescent spurt has significance for proficiency in sports skills. Clearly, boys who reach adolescence at an early age are generally quite different in size, physique, or performance compared with boys who reach adolescence later. Further, adolescent growth and maturation do not occur in a social vacuum. Individual variations in the timing of the adolescent growth spurt, including spurts in size, performance, and sexual maturation, as well as associated changes in behavior, are the backdrop against which youths evaluate and interpret their own growth, maturation, and social status among peers. Proficiency in physical performance is a significant component of the self-evaluative process for many adolescent boys, and also helps determine social status within the adolescent group. Hence, the individuality of the timing of changes occurring during male adolescence should be recognized and appreciated, especially by those who work with boys in the context of youth sports programs. More comprehensive discussions of the significance of growth- and maturity-associated variation in youth sports are presented by Malina (1988a, 1988b, in press).

Given the current interest in regular physical activity during growth as a potentially significant factor in the prevention of cardiovascular disease, the role of habitual physical activity during adolescence merits more detailed consideration.

The evidence, though largely cross-sectional, suggests a trend toward a decline in the level of physical activity during adolescence, especially in later adolescence and more so in boys than in girls (Malina, 1986c). The decline may be related to the social demands of adolescence and perhaps to career choices, that is, the transition from school to work. It would thus be of interest to consider changes in habitual physical activity relative to the timing of the adolescent growth spurt to see whether individual variation in timing is a significant factor.

Finally, the dramatic changes in size, proportion, and motor performance during adolescence result in an altered bodily configuration and performance capacity. These changes may have significant behavioral correlates. The adolescent's body image is probably revised, especially in terms of physical appearance, limits of strength, and coordination. Variation in the timing of growth and maturational events of adolescence adds to the complexity of the changing relationships between body image and behavior during this phase of development. Thus it would be of interest to consider longitudinally the association between biological and behavioral changes during normal adolescence. Furthermore, the changes in somatic characteristics and motor performance contribute largely to adult sexual dimorphism, which becomes apparent at this time. Although some of the sexually dimorphic characteristics may have lost their original function, they certainly serve as releasers of mating behavior in a variety of cultures (Tanner, 1981), and in this regard may also have an important influence on behavior.

# Summary

The growth and motor performance of Belgian boys followed longitudinally between 12 and 19 years of age are reported. Data are based on 270 to 300 boys observed annually over 5 years, at six observation points, and include 16 somatic and 7 motor characteristics. In addition to size and performance attained at specific ages, growth velocities for all variables and ages at the adolescent spurt for most variables (some did not show a clear spurt) were estimated with nonsmoothed polynomials. Although there are several limitations to the procedures used to estimate ages at and velocities of the growth spurt in anthropometric and performance characteristics, the following summarize the major observations of the analysis.

1. Body weight, height, segment lengths, trunk breadths, and circumferences show a maximum velocity of growth between 14.0 and 15.0 years of age. Allowing for variation in methods of estimating the adolescent growth spurt in height among different longitudinal studies, the estimated age at the height spurt and peak height velocity in Belgian boys (14.2 years and 9.2 cm/year, respectively) compare well with those for several samples of European boys (13.8 to 14.4 years and 8.2 to 10.3 cm/year, respectively).

2. The distance and velocity of growth in skinfold thicknesses differ from other anthropometric dimensions. Skinfolds on the trunk increase in thickness during adolescence, while those on the extremities decrease in thickness. Velocities of the triceps and calf skinfolds increase in early adolescence, but then decline and eventually become negative by 14.5 to 15.0 years. Velocities of the subscapular and suprailiac skinfolds are positive and reasonably constant during the growth spurt, but later in adolescence (16 to 18 years), velocities of the two trunk skin-

folds differ. Those for the subscapular skinfold increase slightly while those for the suprailiac skinfold decline considerably.

3. When anthropometric dimensions are aligned on the timing of the height spurt or the weight spurt, skeletal lengths and trunk breadths are synchronized better with the height spurt whereas limb circumferences are synchronized better with the weight spurt. The magnitudes of the spurts in other anthropometric dimensions except the skinfolds do not vary with alignment on either the height spurt or the weight spurt.

4. Velocities of the extremity skinfolds begin to decline 2 to 3 years before the height spurt or weight spurt. Velocities of the triceps skinfold reach a nadir about 1.5 to 2 years after the spurts and then increase. Velocities of the calf skinfold reach a nadir 3 years after the spurts, but changes after this time cannot be detected in the analysis. Velocities of the subscapular skinfold are rather constant both before and after the height or weight spurts, while those for the suprailiac skinfold increase slightly prior to the height or weight spurts and then decline markedly. The decline appears to occur at or just after the height or weight spurts, and continues 3 years after the spurts.

5. The three strength tests (static, functional, explosive) show velocity curves that are qualitatively similar to those for height and weight. Their adolescent spurts occur after the height spurt and more coincident with the weight spurt. As would be expected, the spurts in the three strength tests align closely with the spurt in arm pull (static) strength.

6. Flexibility and the two speed tests appear to reach maximum velocities prior to the height and weight spurts.

7. Median velocities for all motor items are positive during the adolescent spurt, with no indication of a period of adolescent awkwardness or of an overgrown, clumsy age. There is also no indication that the adolescent boy outgrows his strength during the growth spurt.

8. In this analysis, not all variables showed clear evidence of an adolescent spurt. For the six variables for which an adolescent spurt and the age at the spurt could be calculated, correlations among the estimated magnitudes of the spurts in height, sitting height, leg length, weight, chest circumference at inspiration, and static strength range from low to moderate (0.10 to 0.59), while correlations among estimated ages at the spurts in each variable are higher (0.23 to 0.69). In contrast, correlations between the magnitude of the spurt and the age at the spurt in each variable approach zero.

# Appendix A

## Description of Anthropometric Techniques

The description of measurement procedures is modified after Renson et al. (1980).

1. *Body weight* was measured with a spring scale accurate to 0.5 kg. The subject wore only his underwear or a bathing suit.

2. *Standing height* was measured with a Martin anthropometer. The subject was in bare feet and stood with his back against a vertical wall, and his heels together touching the wall. The boy's head was in the Frankfurt plane. The sliding end of the anthropometer was placed on the vertex of the head with firm pressure to compress the hair. Height was measured to the nearest millimeter.

3. *Sitting height* was measured with the subject seated on a seat 40 cm high with his feet together. The head and trunk were positioned as for standing height. With the anthropometer placed on the seat behind the subject, the distance from the seat to vertex was measured. Sitting height was measured to the nearest millimeter.

4. *Leg length* was estimated as the difference between standing height and sitting height to the nearest millimeter.

5. *Reaching height* was measured as the maximum height the boy could reach with his feet together and flat on the floor. Both arms with fingers extended were vertically extended above the head; the point of highest reach was recorded to the nearest centimeter. This measurement is a part of the vertical jump testing procedure (see Appendix B).

6. *Biacromial breadth* was measured with a spreading caliper as the distance between the outer edges of the acromial processes. The subject stood in a relaxed position (i.e., not with the shoulders rigid as in a military posture). The measurement was taken to the nearest 0.5 cm.

7. *Chest breadth* was taken with a spreading caliper as the distance between the two most lateral points of the rib cage at mesosternal level with the subject standing in a relaxed position. The caliper was held in a horizontal plane and the arm of the caliper positioned on the nearest rib. The measurement was taken to the nearest 0.5 cm.

8. *Biepicondylar breadth of the humerus* was measured as the distance between the epicondyles of the left humerus. The subject stood in a relaxed position with the elbow flexed at a right angle. This measurement was taken with a spreading caliper to the nearest millimeter.

9. *Bicondylar breadth of the femur* was measured with a spreading caliper as the distance between the lateral aspects of the condyles of the left femur. The measurement was taken to the nearest millimeter.

10. *Chest circumference at inspiration* was measured with the plastic tape placed under the tips of the scapular posteriorly and over the nipples anteriorly. The tape was held firmly and the subject was asked to make a complete inspiration. The measurement was taken to the nearest millimeter.

11. *Thigh circumference* was measured with the subject standing with his feet slightly apart and his weight evenly distributed on both feet. The measurement was taken horizontally as a maximal circumference of the left thigh just below the gluteal fold. The measurement was taken to the nearest millimeter.

12. *Calf circumference* was measured with subject standing in the same position as for thigh circumference. The measurement was taken as the maximum circumference of the left calf to the nearest millimeter.

13. *Flexed upper arm circumference* was measured with the subject standing relaxed and his left arm flexed maximally. The measurement was taken to the nearest millimeter as the maximum circumference over the flexed biceps brachii muscle.

14. *Triceps skinfold* was measured over the triceps brachii muscle of the relaxed left arm at a level midway between the acromial and olecranon processes. This skinfold and all others were measured with a Harpenden skinfold caliper to the nearest 0.1 millimeter.

15. *Calf skinfold* was measured at the level of the left triceps surae muscle just below the popliteal area.

16. *Subscapular skinfold* was measured just below the angle of the left scapula with the fold following the natural cleavage line of the skin.

17. *Suprailiac skinfold* was measured approximately 1 cm above and 2 cm medial to the left superior iliac spine, in a line running parallel to the natural cleavage line of the skin.

# Appendix B

## Description of Leuven Motor Ability Tests

The description of tests is modified after Renson et al. (1980).

### Stick Balance[1]

*Factor: Eye-hand coordination*
*Material*
- A 2 cm x 2 cm aluminum tube, 30 cm long and closed at both ends with a rubber stopper.

*Instructions for the Subject*
Take a comfortable position. Using the left or the right hand, try to balance the stick on your pointer finger for as long as possible. The hand should be closed with the pointer stretched. The stick may not touch the body and the feet may not move. To start you may hold the stick upright with the opposite hand. When you take that hand away the test will begin. The test ends if the stick touches the body, falls, or if the feet move. The test is done three times with the best result taken as the score.

*Directions for the Test Leader*
- The test leader should place himself/herself at the side of the subject.
- The subject is allowed one trial to become familiar with the test and to make sure that the instructions are understood.
- After this trial the test is carried out three times.
- The stick must be placed on the palm side of the distal phalanx of the left or right pointer finger.
- The stopwatch is started when the supporting hand is removed from the stick.

*Score*
The score is given as the best of three trials in 10ths of a second.

### Plate Tapping

*Factor: Speed of Limb Movement*
*Material*
- Two plates, each 20 cm in diameter, are horizontally fixed 60 cm apart at the same level on a single support. The plates are set at the level of the iliac (hip)

---

[1]The Stick Balance Test was not included in the analysis.

crests. A photo cell connected to a counter is set between the two plates. The number of times that the light ray is broken by the passing of the hand is then recorded on the counter.
* Stopwatch.

### Instructions for the Subject

Take a place in front of the table with a slightly spread stance. Your preferred hand is placed on the disc opposite this hand. You must move your preferred hand back and forth between the two discs as quickly as possible. Be sure to touch the discs each time. When I say "ready ...'start!" you will begin moving your preferred hand back and forth as quickly as possible during 20 seconds. DO NOT stop before I give the signal "stop!" While you are performing, I will count aloud. The test is performed once.

### Directions for the Test Leader

* The test leader should stand at the side of the subject.
* In preparation for the test, set the right hand of a right-handed subject on the left plate (left hand of a left-handed subject on the right plate). The test leader must check that the right shoulder of a right-handed subject is positioned roughly in the middle between the two plates (for left-handed subjects the opposite).
* The stopwatch is started at the signal "ready ... start!" and stopped after 20 seconds with the signal "stop!"
* When an electronic apparatus is not available, an assistant should count the number of taps. It may also be simpler to count the number of taps on one plate and double this. The number on nontaps is then subtracted in each case. The test leader keeps the time and encourages the subject.
* The subject does not have to tap the plates hard. It is only important to move back and forth quickly.

### Score

The score is recorded as the total number of taps on each of the plates in 20 seconds. This is therefore the total correct taps on one plate multiplied by 2.

## Sit and Reach

### Factor: Flexibility
### Material

* A test table or box with the following dimensions: length 35 cm, width 45 cm, height 32 cm. The top plate is 55 cm long and 45 cm wide. This top plate extends 15 cm over the side supporting the feet. A scale from 0 to 50 cm is drawn on the top plate with tape by means of parallel lines every centimeter.

### Instructions for the Subject

Sit down. Place your feet flat against the box. Bend at the trunk as far forward as possible without bending your knees and with the hands stretched out in front of you. Try to remain still in the farthest position. Use no bouncing movements. The test will be done twice, with the better result counting as the score.

### Directions for the Test Leader

* The tester stands at the side of the subject and fixes his/her knees in the extended position.

- The score is determined as the farthest position the subject can reach on the scale with his/her fingertips. The subject must hold this position at least for a count or two so that the tester can correctly read the score.
- When the fingers of each hand do not reach an equal position, the average distance of the two fingertips is taken.
- The test must be done slowly and progressively without any bouncing movements.
- The second trial follows after a short rest period.

### Score
The better result of the two trials is recorded. The score is given in centimeters reached on the scale on the top of the box.

## Vertical Jump

### Factor: Explosive strength
### Material
- A blackboard 200 cm high and 60 cm wide is fixed on the wall 155 cm above the ground. The board is divided by horizontal lines placed 5 cm apart. The exact height above the ground is written on the board every 10 cm in order to facilitate the reading of the results.
- Chalk (best choice is magnesium chalk).

### Instructions for the Subject
Cover the fingertips of both hands with chalk. Stand in front of the board with both hands stretched above the head. The feet should be together flat on the floor. With your body, arms, and fingers fully stretched, make a mark with fingertips on the board. Now stand sidewards next to the board, facing either left or right. Bend your knees, swing your arms, and jump as high as possible. At the highest point, touch the board with the fingertips of the left or right hand. The test is done three times and the best result is taken.

### Directions for the Test Leader
Reaching height
- The tester stands behind the subject and helps him/her assume the correct position.
- Check if the feet are flat on the floor while the entire body is stretched.
- The reaching height is registered in centimeters and is measured only once.
- Horizontal lines are drawn on the board 5 cm apart.
- Results that fall between the lines are estimated (with the eye) to the nearest centimeter.
- If the reach of the fingertips of both hands is not equal, ask the subject to make it so. If this is not possible, then take the mean height of the fingertips of the two hands.
Jumping height
- Depending on whether the subject is right- or left-handed, he/she takes a place with the right or left side facing the board.
- Emphasis should be placed on bending the knees, swinging the arms, complete stretching of the body, and marking the board at the highest point.
- No steps may be taken before the jump.

- During the jump, take a position far enough from the subject and note exactly where the board is touched.
- Each subject has three attempts, and the best effort in centimeters is taken as the score.
- Results that fall between the lines are also estimated to the nearest centimeter by the naked eye.
- The chalk marks on the board should be erased regularly.

### Score
The score is taken as the difference between the reaching height and the best of the three vertical jumps.

## Arm Pull

### Factor: Static strength
### Material
- A calibrated dynamometer with a removable backpiece is fixed to a vertical support (e.g., at a wall bar or a vertical pole) by means of a chain and a snap link. Both the height and the length of the pulling device must be adjustable. The chain is fixed so that the hand grip of the dynamometer can be adjusted in the plane of the elbow pit of the supporting arm. An indicator needle on the scale of the dynamometer indicates the maximum result. Two additional supporting grips are provided on the right and left side at the vertical support. These are used to stabilize the arm not being tested (nonpreferred arm).

### Instructions for the Subject
Stand sidewards with the feet spread. While you support yourself against the board with a horizontally stretched arm, take the hand grip with the preferred arm. Pull as hard as possible, as if you were bending a bow. Do not jerk the chain.

### Directions for the Test Leader
- The tester places himself/herself in front of the subject and adjusts the chain so that the hand grip lies in the plane of the elbow pit of the supporting arm. The arm not being tested (right/left) grips the vertical support (right/left) at shoulder height.
- The subject should pull not only with the arm muscles but, more important, with the back muscles as well.
- Check that the subject takes a steady position with feet spread.
- Before the test is taken, the tester must make sure that the dynamometer is set at zero and that the snap link and chain are well secured.
- After a short rest, a second attempt is made.
- The indicator needle is not returned to zero after the first attempt. So the tester has only to check if the second attempt is better than the first.

### Score
The better result from the two attempts is taken as the score. The result is read to the nearest 0.5 kg.

## Leg Lifts

*Factor: Trunk strength*
*Material*
- 2 mats (set lengthwise next to each other);
- Stopwatch.

### Instructions for the Subject
Lie down on your back on the mat with the legs extended and the hands under the neck. First lift both legs up to 90° until they touch my hand. This is the correct position. Let the legs back down. When I say "start," lift your two stretched legs up as quickly as possible until they touch my hand. Do this as many times as possible in 20 seconds. The legs must return each time to the floor. The legs must remain stretched, and try to keep the pelvis on the ground. Continue these movements as quickly as possible until I say "stop!"

### Directions for the Test Leader
- The test leader kneels next to the subject and holds his/her left hand above the pelvis of the subject so that when the subject lifts the legs until they touch the hand, they will form a 90° angle with the trunk.
- The test leader holds his/her hand at about the height of the knee of the subject.
- The back and shoulders must remain against the ground during the entire test. The help of an assistant is necessary here; the assistant's body weight can help fix the upper arms of the subject to the floor.
- The test leader indicates out loud each time the legs of the subject touch the mat. Thus, a complete movement includes the lifting of the legs, the touching of the hand, and the return of the legs to the mat.
- After the instructions are given and before the test begins, the subject should execute the entire movement one time slowly while the test leader reminds him/her (a) to lift the legs completely until they touch the test leader's hand, (b) to return his/her legs each time to the mat, and (c) to keep legs extended at all times.
- The watch is started at the signal "ready ... start!" and the test begins.
- The watch is stopped after 20 seconds.
- The test leader should continually give the correct count aloud.
- Incorrect movements are not counted.
- The test leader must check and see that the legs are lifted to 90°. It may be necessary to move his/her hand during the test if the position of the subject changes. These shifting movements must be limited as much as possible by the assistant who is pressing on the upper arms of the subject.
- The pelvis may be slightly raised above the floor to allow a correct movement.

### Score
The total number of times that the correct movement is completed in 20 seconds is taken as the score.

## Bent Arm Hang

*Factor: Functional strength*
*Material*
- A horizontal bar with a diameter of 2.5 cm set ±190 cm above the ground;
- Stopwatch.

### Instructions for the Subject
Take a position under the bar and place your hands on the bar at shoulder width in a forward grip. Lift yourself up until your chin is above the bar. Hold this position as long as possible without resting your chin on the bar. The test is finished when you lower yourself so that the eyes are below the bar.

### Directions for the Test Leader
- Let the subject stand under the bar with hands in a forward grip on the bar at shoulder width. Be careful—most subjects place the hands too far apart.
- Adjust the height of the bar to the mean reaching height of the test group.
- With the watch ready in the hand, take the subject by the hips and lift him/her into the correct position.
- Start the watch the moment the subject's chin is above the bar and the tester lets him/her go.
- The tester should stop the swinging movements of the subject. The tester should encourage the subject.
- Stop the watch when the subject cannot hold the required position any longer, as described above (eyes below the bar).
- Do not tell the time to the subject during the test.

### Score
The time in 10ths of a second is taken as the score.

## Shuttle run, 50 m

*Factor: Running speed*
*Material*
- Slip-proof floor;
- Stopwatch;
- Measuring tape;
- Chalk or white tape;
- Traffic cones.

### Instructions for the Subject
Get in a ready position behind the line. One foot should be just behind the line. When the start is given, run as quickly as possible to the other line and cross it with both feet. Turn around as quickly as possible, return to the starting line, and cross that with both feet. This is one cycle, and it must be completed five times. On the fifth time, do not slow down when coming to the finish but continue running. This test is done once.

### Directions for the Test Leader
- Two parallel lines are made on the floor (chalk or tape) 5 m apart.

- The line is 120 cm long and the ends of each line are marked with cones (Indian clubs, blocks, etc.).
- The tester should make sure that the subject crosses the line with both feet, that he/she remains in the required path, and that the turns are made as quickly as possible.
- After each cycle the number of cycles completed should be called aloud.
- The watch is stopped when the subject crosses the finish line with one foot.
- The subject may not slip or slide during the test. Therefore a slip-proof floor is necessary.

*Score*
The time needed to complete five cycles is taken as the score and written in 10ths of a second.

# Appendix C

## Estimation of Growth Velocities

### Second-Degree Polynomial With Three Observations

The three measurements are equally spaced in time. Therefore, the time ($t$) may be denoted as $t = -1$, $0$, and $+1$, and the three observations ($X$) as $X = X_{-1}$, $X_0$, and $X_1$. The velocity in the midpoint ($t = 0$) is required. The growth curve $g(t)$ through the points is given by $g(t) = at^2 + bt + c$. The velocity curve $V(t)$ after differentiation is $V(t) = 2at + b$. The velocity in the midpoint is $V(0) = b$.

Given the measurements, the following system of equations may be written:

$$\left.\begin{array}{l} X_{-1} = a - b + c \\ X_0 = c \\ X_1 = a + b + c \end{array}\right\} \quad \left.\begin{array}{l} -a + b = X_0 - X_{-1} = \delta_1 \\ a + b = X_1 - X_0 = \delta_2 \end{array}\right\} \quad 2b = \delta_1 + \delta_2$$

Thus, $V(0) = b = (\delta_1 + \delta_2)/2$ in which $\delta_1$ and $\delta_2$ are the two increments.

### Third-Degree Polynomial With Four Observations

The four measurements are equally spaced in time. The velocity is required in the middle of the time interval. Time may be denoted by $t = -1.5$, $-.5$, $.5$, and $1.5$. The four observations are $X = X_{-1.5}$, $X_{-.5}$, $X_{.5}$, and $X_{1.5}$. The growth curve $g(t)$ through the points is given by $g(t) = at^3 + bt^2 + ct + d$. The velocity curve $V(t)$ after differentiation of $g(t)$ is $V(t) = 3at^2 + 2bt + c$. The velocity in the middle of the time interval ($t = 0$) is $V(0) = c$.

Given the observations, the following system of equations may be written using $\delta_1$, $\delta_2$, and $\delta_3$ as the successive increments between the four points.

$$\left.\begin{array}{l} X_{-1.5} = -27/8\,a + 9/4\,b - 3/2\,c + d \\ X_{1.5} = 27/8\,a + 9/4\,b + 3/2\,c + d \end{array}\right\} \begin{array}{l} X_{1.5} - X_{-1.5} = \\ 27/4\,a + 3\,c = \delta_1 + \delta_2 + \delta_3 \end{array}$$

$$\left.\begin{array}{l} X_{-.5} = -1/8\,a + 1/4\,b - 1/2\,c + d \\ X_{.5} = 1/8\,a + 1/4\,b + 1/2\,c + d \end{array}\right\} X_{.5} - X_{-.5} = 1/4\,a + c = \delta_2$$

This leads to $27\,\delta_2 - (\delta_1 + \delta_2 + \delta_3) = 24\,c$, or

$$V(0) = [24\,\delta_2 + (\delta_2 - \delta_1) + (\delta_2 - \delta_3)]/24 = \delta_2 + \frac{\delta_2 - \delta_1}{24} + \frac{\delta_2 - \delta_3}{24}$$

# Appendix D

## Number of Subjects and the Size and Performance Attained at Each Chronological Age From 12.5 to 18.0 Years

**Table D1   Weight (kg)**

| Age (years) | N | M | SD | Median | Minimum | Maximum |
|---|---|---|---|---|---|---|
| 12.5 | 171 | 38.6 | 6.2 | 37.7 | 27.0 | 63.0 |
| 13.0 | 274 | 41.2 | 7.3 | 40.0 | 29.0 | 79.5 |
| 13.5 | 274 | 43.4 | 7.7 | 42.2 | 30.5 | 83.2 |
| 14.0 | 274 | 46.1 | 8.1 | 45.0 | 32.7 | 87.0 |
| 14.5 | 274 | 49.2 | 8.5 | 48.5 | 34.0 | 89.7 |
| 15.0 | 274 | 52.3 | 8.7 | 51.5 | 36.5 | 92.5 |
| 15.5 | 274 | 55.5 | 8.7 | 54.5 | 39.0 | 89.7 |
| 16.0 | 274 | 58.4 | 8.7 | 58.0 | 41.2 | 97.0 |
| 16.5 | 274 | 61.0 | 8.6 | 60.5 | 43.0 | 98.7 |
| 17.0 | 274 | 63.0 | 8.6 | 62.5 | 44.7 | 100.5 |
| 17.5 | 245 | 64.6 | 8.6 | 64.5 | 45.5 | 103.2 |
| 18.0 | 103 | 66.7 | 9.0 | 66.0 | 51.0 | 106.0 |

**Table D2   Height (cm)**

| Age (years) | N | M | SD | Median | Minimum | Maximum |
|---|---|---|---|---|---|---|
| 12.5 | 172 | 148.8 | 6.2 | 148.9 | 134.2 | 165.0 |
| 13.0 | 276 | 151.3 | 6.1 | 151.2 | 135.5 | 167.8 |
| 13.5 | 276 | 154.0 | 6.4 | 153.6 | 137.2 | 170.8 |
| 14.0 | 276 | 157.4 | 6.9 | 156.9 | 139.0 | 175.6 |
| 14.5 | 276 | 161.2 | 7.4 | 160.9 | 142.0 | 180.6 |
| 15.0 | 276 | 165.2 | 7.4 | 165.3 | 145.1 | 184.2 |
| 15.5 | 276 | 168.8 | 7.0 | 169.0 | 149.8 | 187.8 |
| 16.0 | 276 | 171.6 | 6.5 | 171.8 | 154.5 | 189.7 |
| 16.5 | 276 | 173.5 | 6.1 | 173.3 | 157.7 | 191.6 |
| 17.0 | 276 | 174.8 | 5.9 | 174.7 | 159.4 | 192.6 |
| 17.5 | 247 | 175.7 | 5.7 | 175.5 | 160.4 | 194.2 |
| 18.0 | 104 | 176.5 | 5.4 | 176.0 | 165.6 | 190.9 |

**Table D3   Sitting height (cm)**

| Age (years) | N | M | SD | Median | Minimum | Maximum |
|---|---|---|---|---|---|---|
| 12.5 | 167 | 76.8 | 3.1 | 76.7 | 68.6 | 84.3 |
| 13.0 | 271 | 77.9 | 3.1 | 77.7 | 69.6 | 85.8 |
| 13.5 | 271 | 79.1 | 3.1 | 79.1 | 70.6 | 88.4 |
| 14.0 | 271 | 80.8 | 3.3 | 80.8 | 72.8 | 90.3 |
| 14.5 | 271 | 82.7 | 3.6 | 82.7 | 71.6 | 92.2 |
| 15.0 | 271 | 84.7 | 3.7 | 84.6 | 74.9 | 94.4 |
| 15.5 | 271 | 86.6 | 3.6 | 86.6 | 78.0 | 96.7 |
| 16.0 | 271 | 88.2 | 3.4 | 88.3 | 78.5 | 96.6 |
| 16.5 | 271 | 89.5 | 3.1 | 89.7 | 81.1 | 97.6 |
| 17.0 | 271 | 90.4 | 3.0 | 90.3 | 83.2 | 98.3 |
| 17.5 | 244 | 90.9 | 2.8 | 90.5 | 83.7 | 99.0 |
| 18.0 | 104 | 91.3 | 2.9 | 91.0 | 85.3 | 99.0 |

**Table D4    Leg length (cm)**

| Age (years) | N | M | SD | Median | Minimum | Maximum |
|---|---|---|---|---|---|---|
| 12.5 | 167 | 72.1 | 4.1 | 71.9 | 62.2 | 82.0 |
| 13.0 | 271 | 73.5 | 4.0 | 73.4 | 62.4 | 83.5 |
| 13.5 | 271 | 75.0 | 4.1 | 74.7 | 64.1 | 85.6 |
| 14.0 | 271 | 76.7 | 4.3 | 76.3 | 65.9 | 87.6 |
| 14.5 | 271 | 78.6 | 4.5 | 78.3 | 67.3 | 89.8 |
| 15.0 | 271 | 80.5 | 4.5 | 80.5 | 68.7 | 91.8 |
| 15.5 | 271 | 82.2 | 4.3 | 82.1 | 71.2 | 92.8 |
| 16.0 | 271 | 83.4 | 4.1 | 83.2 | 73.7 | 94.2 |
| 16.5 | 271 | 84.0 | 4.0 | 83.8 | 74.5 | 95.1 |
| 17.0 | 271 | 84.4 | 4.0 | 84.2 | 74.5 | 96.0 |
| 17.5 | 244 | 84.8 | 4.0 | 84.6 | 73.8 | 95.5 |
| 18.0 | 104 | 85.1 | 3.7 | 84.7 | 76.6 | 95.9 |

**Table D5    Biacromial breadth (cm)**

| Age (years) | N | M | SD | Median | Minimum | Maximum |
|---|---|---|---|---|---|---|
| 12.5 | 171 | 32.3 | 1.8 | 32.0 | 28.0 | 37.0 |
| 13.0 | 274 | 32.7 | 1.8 | 32.7 | 28.5 | 38.0 |
| 13.5 | 274 | 33.0 | 1.8 | 33.0 | 27.0 | 37.5 |
| 14.0 | 274 | 33.6 | 1.9 | 33.5 | 28.0 | 38.7 |
| 14.5 | 274 | 34.6 | 2.0 | 34.5 | 29.0 | 40.5 |
| 15.0 | 274 | 35.8 | 2.1 | 36.0 | 30.5 | 42.5 |
| 15.5 | 274 | 36.9 | 2.1 | 37.0 | 31.7 | 43.0 |
| 16.0 | 274 | 37.6 | 2.0 | 37.5 | 32.0 | 43.0 |
| 16.5 | 274 | 38.0 | 2.0 | 38.0 | 32.5 | 43.0 |
| 17.0 | 274 | 38.4 | 1.9 | 38.5 | 33.0 | 43.7 |
| 17.5 | 245 | 38.9 | 1.8 | 39.0 | 34.5 | 44.5 |
| 18.0 | 103 | 39.4 | 1.5 | 39.5 | 36.0 | 42.5 |

**Table D6    Chest breadth (cm)**

| Age (years) | N | M | SD | Median | Minimum | Maximum |
|---|---|---|---|---|---|---|
| 12.5 | 171 | 23.6 | 1.6 | 23.5 | 20.0 | 29.0 |
| 13.0 | 272 | 24.1 | 1.6 | 24.0 | 20.5 | 31.0 |
| 13.5 | 272 | 24.5 | 1.6 | 24.5 | 20.5 | 31.5 |
| 14.0 | 272 | 24.9 | 1.7 | 25.0 | 21.0 | 32.0 |
| 14.5 | 272 | 25.4 | 1.7 | 25.5 | 21.0 | 31.0 |
| 15.0 | 272 | 26.3 | 1.9 | 26.2 | 22.0 | 32.7 |
| 15.5 | 272 | 27.3 | 1.9 | 27.2 | 23.0 | 34.5 |
| 16.0 | 272 | 28.0 | 1.9 | 28.0 | 23.5 | 33.7 |
| 16.5 | 272 | 28.5 | 1.9 | 28.5 | 24.0 | 33.0 |
| 17.0 | 272 | 28.9 | 1.8 | 29.0 | 24.5 | 34.0 |
| 17.5 | 243 | 29.1 | 1.8 | 29.0 | 24.0 | 34.0 |
| 18.0 | 101 | 29.5 | 1.7 | 29.5 | 26.0 | 34.0 |

**Table D7    Biepicondylar humerus breadth (mm)**

| Age (years) | N | M | SD | Median | Minimum | Maximum |
|---|---|---|---|---|---|---|
| 12.5 | 163 | 60.8 | 3.5 | 61 | 50 | 68 |
| 13.0 | 265 | 61.9 | 3.5 | 62 | 53 | 71 |
| 13.5 | 265 | 63.6 | 3.7 | 63 | 54 | 74 |
| 14.0 | 265 | 64.3 | 3.7 | 64 | 55 | 74 |
| 14.5 | 265 | 64.6 | 3.7 | 65 | 54 | 73 |
| 15.0 | 265 | 66.2 | 3.9 | 66 | 55 | 75 |
| 15.5 | 265 | 68.6 | 3.7 | 69 | 59 | 79 |
| 16.0 | 265 | 69.8 | 3.5 | 70 | 59 | 78 |
| 16.5 | 265 | 69.7 | 3.3 | 70 | 60 | 78 |
| 17.0 | 265 | 69.5 | 3.3 | 70 | 60 | 79 |
| 17.5 | 239 | 69.2 | 3.3 | 69 | 59 | 78 |
| 18.0 | 102 | 69.1 | 3.6 | 69 | 58 | 79 |

**Table D8    Bicondylar femur breadth (mm)**

| Age (years) | N | M | SD | Median | Minimum | Maximum |
|---|---|---|---|---|---|---|
| 12.5 | 168 | 89.7 | 5.4 | 89 | 79 | 107 |
| 13.0 | 267 | 91.2 | 5.6 | 91 | 79 | 122 |
| 13.5 | 267 | 92.3 | 5.6 | 92 | 80 | 122 |
| 14.0 | 267 | 93.1 | 5.7 | 93 | 79 | 122 |
| 14.5 | 267 | 94.3 | 5.7 | 94 | 81 | 120 |
| 15.0 | 267 | 95.7 | 5.6 | 95 | 79 | 118 |
| 15.5 | 267 | 97.2 | 5.6 | 97 | 83 | 117 |
| 16.0 | 267 | 96.9 | 5.5 | 97 | 85 | 117 |
| 16.5 | 267 | 95.7 | 5.1 | 95 | 85 | 113 |
| 17.0 | 267 | 95.5 | 4.6 | 95 | 85 | 110 |
| 17.5 | 240 | 96.0 | 4.5 | 96 | 86 | 109 |
| 18.0 | 99 | 96.4 | 5.0 | 96 | 86 | 110 |


**Table D9    Chest circumference inspiration (cm)**

| Age (years) | N | M | SD | Median | Minimum | Maximum |
|---|---|---|---|---|---|---|
| 12.5 | 166 | 74.9 | 4.2 | 74.5 | 66.0 | 90.0 |
| 13.0 | 270 | 76.6 | 5.0 | 76.0 | 67.0 | 102.0 |
| 13.5 | 270 | 78.1 | 5.2 | 77.5 | 68.0 | 105.0 |
| 14.0 | 270 | 80.0 | 5.5 | 79.5 | 69.5 | 108.0 |
| 14.5 | 270 | 82.3 | 5.5 | 8?.0 | 70.0 | 106.7 |
| 15.0 | 270 | 84.7 | 5.4 | 84.5 | 72.2 | 105.5 |
| 15.5 | 270 | 87.1 | 5.2 | 87.0 | 74.5 | 106.2 |
| 16.0 | 270 | 89.1 | 5.1 | 89.0 | 77.0 | 109.0 |
| 16.5 | 270 | 90.8 | 5.0 | 91.0 | 77.0 | 110.0 |
| 17.0 | 270 | 92.3 | 5.0 | 92.0 | 78.5 | 111.0 |
| 17.5 | 241 | 93.6 | 5.0 | 93.5 | 80.0 | 111.0 |
| 18.0 | 104 | 94.8 | 5.1 | 95.0 | 84.0 | 111.0 |

## Table D10    Flexed arm circumference (cm)

| Age (years) | N | M | SD | Median | Minimum | Maximum |
|---|---|---|---|---|---|---|
| 12.5 | 169 | 21.8 | 1.9 | 22.0 | 18.0 | 29.0 |
| 13.0 | 271 | 22.3 | 2.2 | 22.0 | 17.0 | 31.0 |
| 13.5 | 271 | 22.6 | 2.3 | 22.2 | 17.7 | 32.0 |
| 14.0 | 271 | 23.2 | 2.4 | 23.0 | 18.0 | 33.0 |
| 14.5 | 271 | 23.9 | 2.4 | 24.0 | 17.5 | 32.7 |
| 15.0 | 271 | 24.8 | 2.4 | 24.5 | 18.5 | 32.5 |
| 15.5 | 271 | 25.6 | 2.4 | 25.5 | 19.5 | 33.5 |
| 16.0 | 271 | 26.4 | 2.4 | 26.2 | 20.0 | 35.5 |
| 16.5 | 271 | 27.1 | 2.5 | 27.0 | 21.0 | 36.0 |
| 17.0 | 271 | 27.6 | 2.4 | 27.5 | 21.7 | 36.5 |
| 17.5 | 242 | 27.9 | 2.5 | 27.5 | 22.2 | 36.5 |
| 18.0 | 102 | 28.1 | 2.5 | 28.0 | 22.5 | 35.0 |

## Table D11    Thigh circumference (cm)

| Age (years) | N | M | SD | Median | Minimum | Maximum |
|---|---|---|---|---|---|---|
| 12.5 | 168 | 41.8 | 3.7 | 41.5 | 34.0 | 56.5 |
| 13.0 | 269 | 42.6 | 4.3 | 42.0 | 34.0 | 61.5 |
| 13.5 | 269 | 43.1 | 4.2 | 43.0 | 34.0 | 60.2 |
| 14.0 | 269 | 44.2 | 4.2 | 44.0 | 35.0 | 59.0 |
| 14.5 | 269 | 45.7 | 4.1 | 45.0 | 37.0 | 59.7 |
| 15.0 | 269 | 46.7 | 4.0 | 46.5 | 39.0 | 62.0 |
| 15.5 | 269 | 47.4 | 3.8 | 47.0 | 39.2 | 61.5 |
| 16.0 | 269 | 48.5 | 3.8 | 48.7 | 39.0 | 63.0 |
| 16.5 | 269 | 49.8 | 3.8 | 49.7 | 40.2 | 64.0 |
| 17.0 | 269 | 50.8 | 3.8 | 50.7 | 41.0 | 65.0 |
| 17.5 | 241 | 51.6 | 4.0 | 51.5 | 42.0 | 67.0 |
| 18.0 | 101 | 52.5 | 4.5 | 52.5 | 42.0 | 69.0 |

**Table D12    Calf circumference (cm)**

| Age (years) | N | M | SD | Median | Minimum | Maximum |
|---|---|---|---|---|---|---|
| 12.5 | 167 | 29.3 | 2.1 | 29.0 | 25.0 | 37.5 |
| 13.0 | 270 | 29.8 | 2.4 | 29.7 | 25.5 | 40.0 |
| 13.5 | 270 | 30.3 | 2.5 | 30.0 | 25.0 | 41.5 |
| 14.0 | 270 | 31.0 | 2.6 | 31.0 | 26.0 | 43.0 |
| 14.5 | 270 | 31.8 | 2.6 | 31.7 | 26.5 | 43.5 |
| 15.0 | 270 | 32.6 | 2.5 | 32.5 | 27.0 | 44.0 |
| 15.5 | 270 | 33.4 | 2.4 | 33.0 | 28.0 | 43.2 |
| 16.0 | 270 | 33.9 | 2.4 | 33.5 | 29.0 | 44.0 |
| 16.5 | 270 | 34.3 | 2.4 | 34.0 | 29.2 | 44.5 |
| 17.0 | 270 | 34.7 | 2.4 | 34.5 | 29.5 | 45.0 |
| 17.5 | 242 | 35.2 | 2.5 | 35.0 | 30.0 | 44.5 |
| 18.0 | 103 | 35.7 | 2.6 | 35.5 | 31.0 | 44.5 |

**Table D13    Triceps skinfold (log units)**

| Age (years) | N | M | SD | Median | Minimum | Maximum |
|---|---|---|---|---|---|---|
| 12.5 | 167 | 183.5 | 19.9 | 183 | 134 | 238 |
| 13.0 | 268 | 187.2 | 19.8 | 186 | 136 | 252 |
| 13.5 | 268 | 188.2 | 18.7 | 187 | 139 | 246 |
| 14.0 | 268 | 188.3 | 18.8 | 186 | 139 | 243 |
| 14.5 | 268 | 187.7 | 20.2 | 185 | 141 | 246 |
| 15.0 | 268 | 184.8 | 21.0 | 181 | 134 | 255 |
| 15.5 | 268 | 181.1 | 21.9 | 179 | 125 | 251 |
| 16.0 | 268 | 175.0 | 22.8 | 172 | 120 | 248 |
| 16.5 | 268 | 166.6 | 21.7 | 164 | 120 | 246 |
| 17.0 | 268 | 164.7 | 21.4 | 163 | 117 | 245 |
| 17.5 | 240 | 169.6 | 23.3 | 166 | 121 | 259 |
| 18.0 | 101 | 173.5 | 23.1 | 173 | 117 | 249 |

**Table D14    Subscapular skinfold (log units)**

| Age (years) | N | M | SD | Median | Minimum | Maximum |
|---|---|---|---|---|---|---|
| 12.5 | 164 | 157.2 | 19.5 | 153 | 125 | 231 |
| 13.0 | 261 | 161.0 | 22.2 | 157 | 114 | 252 |
| 13.5 | 261 | 163.2 | 21.1 | 159 | 120 | 247 |
| 14.0 | 261 | 165.6 | 19.9 | 163 | 127 | 243 |
| 14.5 | 261 | 168.7 | 19.2 | 165 | 138 | 254 |
| 15.0 | 261 | 170.7 | 18.2 | 168 | 140 | 258 |
| 15.5 | 261 | 171.7 | 17.3 | 169 | 141 | 254 |
| 16.0 | 261 | 173.4 | 16.7 | 171 | 144 | 250 |
| 16.5 | 261 | 175.8 | 16.1 | 173 | 149 | 246 |
| 17.0 | 261 | 178.8 | 15.3 | 177 | 150 | 251 |
| 17.5 | 233 | 181.8 | 14.5 | 180 | 150 | 243 |
| 18.0 | 97 | 185.1 | 14.2 | 183 | 160 | 236 |

**Table D15    Suprailiac skinfold (log units)**

| Age (years) | N | M | SD | Median | Minimum | Maximum |
|---|---|---|---|---|---|---|
| 12.5 | 165 | 136.3 | 24.7 | 132 | 90 | 221 |
| 13.0 | 266 | 143.8 | 27.3 | 138 | 77 | 245 |
| 13.5 | 266 | 149.4 | 26.2 | 144 | 90 | 235 |
| 14.0 | 266 | 155.3 | 25.1 | 151 | 101 | 240 |
| 14.5 | 266 | 161.1 | 25.5 | 157 | 104 | 257 |
| 15.0 | 266 | 165.5 | 25.6 | 161 | 101 | 258 |
| 15.5 | 266 | 169.2 | 24.2 | 166 | 99 | 250 |
| 16.0 | 266 | 173.7 | 22.4 | 170 | 117 | 248 |
| 16.5 | 266 | 177.7 | 21.3 | 174 | 136 | 249 |
| 17.0 | 266 | 177.8 | 21.6 | 174 | 134 | 250 |
| 17.5 | 237 | 176.2 | 21.5 | 174 | 132 | 251 |
| 18.0 | 101 | 177.8 | 20.6 | 176 | 136 | 237 |

Table D16    Calf skinfold (log units)

| Age (years) | N | M | SD | Median | Minimum | Maximum |
|---|---|---|---|---|---|---|
| 12.5 | 168 | 171.8 | 22.8 | 170 | 111 | 242 |
| 13.0 | 271 | 174.0 | 24.0 | 172 | 109 | 249 |
| 13.5 | 271 | 173.3 | 22.6 | 172 | 107 | 241 |
| 14.0 | 271 | 178.3 | 21.1 | 179 | 114 | 229 |
| 14.5 | 271 | 185.9 | 20.8 | 185 | 123 | 243 |
| 15.0 | 271 | 186.0 | 20.7 | 186 | 128 | 258 |
| 15.5 | 271 | 181.0 | 20.3 | 181 | 134 | 256 |
| 16.0 | 271 | 175.1 | 20.1 | 176 | 124 | 254 |
| 16.5 | 271 | 167.9 | 20.5 | 167 | 107 | 234 |
| 17.0 | 271 | 159.1 | 21.3 | 159 | 112 | 240 |
| 17.5 | 242 | 150.8 | 22.0 | 150 | 90 | 222 |
| 18.0 | 103 | 146.6 | 22.9 | 146 | 104 | 219 |

Table D17    Static strength—arm pull (kg)

| Age (years) | N | M | SD | Median | Minimum | Maximum |
|---|---|---|---|---|---|---|
| 12.5 | 140 | 30.8 | 5.8 | 30.0 | 17.0 | 46.5 |
| 13.0 | 219 | 33.0 | 6.4 | 32.5 | 17.0 | 54.0 |
| 13.5 | 219 | 35.7 | 7.4 | 35.0 | 19.0 | 63.0 |
| 14.0 | 219 | 39.4 | 8.6 | 38.5 | 19.0 | 69.5 |
| 14.5 | 219 | 44.6 | 9.8 | 43.5 | 23.5 | 83.0 |
| 15.0 | 219 | 50.5 | 10.6 | 50.0 | 28.5 | 87.7 |
| 15.5 | 219 | 56.4 | 11.4 | 56.0 | 32.0 | 99.5 |
| 16.0 | 219 | 61.5 | 11.8 | 61.0 | 34.7 | 101.5 |
| 16.5 | 219 | 65.5 | 11.9 | 65.0 | 37.2 | 103.0 |
| 17.0 | 219 | 69.0 | 12.0 | 68.5 | 38.0 | 109.5 |
| 17.5 | 194 | 72.3 | 12.7 | 72.5 | 43.2 | 120.0 |
| 18.0 | 79 | 74.0 | 13.7 | 73.0 | 42.5 | 111.0 |

**Table D18   Explosive strength—vertical jump (cm)**

| Age (years) | N | M | SD | Median | Minimum | Maximum |
|---|---|---|---|---|---|---|
| 12.5 | 141 | 32.9 | 4.9 | 33 | 11 | 44 |
| 13.0 | 222 | 33.1 | 4.8 | 33 | 21 | 46 |
| 13.5 | 222 | 34.3 | 5.1 | 35 | 20 | 48 |
| 14.0 | 222 | 35.7 | 5.5 | 36 | 22 | 51 |
| 14.5 | 222 | 37.5 | 5.9 | 37 | 23 | 53 |
| 15.0 | 222 | 39.8 | 6.1 | 39 | 24 | 56 |
| 15.5 | 222 | 42.2 | 6.2 | 42 | 25 | 56 |
| 16.0 | 222 | 44.3 | 6.3 | 44 | 24 | 60 |
| 16.5 | 222 | 46.4 | 6.4 | 46 | 29 | 63 |
| 17.0 | 222 | 47.8 | 6.4 | 48 | 32 | 68 |
| 17.5 | 197 | 48.3 | 6.8 | 48 | 32 | 73 |
| 18.0 | 81 | 48.3 | 7.3 | 47 | 33 | 69 |

**Table D19   Functional strength—bent arm hang (sec)**

| Age (years) | N | M | SD | Median | Minimum | Maximum |
|---|---|---|---|---|---|---|
| 12.5 | 137 | 19.7 | 15.0 | 15.8 | .1 | 91.3 |
| 13.0 | 217 | 18.9 | 14.2 | 16.2 | .1 | 92.3 |
| 13.5 | 217 | 19.8 | 14.8 | 17.2 | .1 | 93.3 |
| 14.0 | 217 | 21.2 | 15.2 | 18.5 | .1 | 82.4 |
| 14.5 | 217 | 23.0 | 15.5 | 20.3 | .1 | 87.5 |
| 15.0 | 217 | 25.5 | 16.5 | 23.4 | .1 | 99.4 |
| 15.5 | 217 | 28.5 | 17.0 | 26.5 | .1 | 111.4 |
| 16.0 | 217 | 31.1 | 17.3 | 29.7 | .1 | 106.8 |
| 16.5 | 217 | 32.9 | 18.0 | 30.6 | .1 | 102.2 |
| 17.0 | 217 | 32.9 | 17.8 | 29.8 | .1 | 96.6 |
| 17.5 | 192 | 32.2 | 18.0 | 29.1 | .1 | 105.6 |
| 18.0 | 80 | 31.8 | 19.0 | 32.3 | .1 | 88.3 |

**Table D20    Trunk strength—leg lifts (#/20 sec)**

| Age (years) | N | M | SD | Median | Minimum | Maximum |
|---|---|---|---|---|---|---|
| 12.5 | 137 | 14.5 | 3.2 | 15 | 3 | 21 |
| 13.0 | 213 | 14.0 | 3.0 | 15 | 1 | 20 |
| 13.5 | 213 | 14.2 | 3.0 | 15 | 1 | 20 |
| 14.0 | 213 | 14.7 | 3.0 | 15 | 1 | 21 |
| 14.5 | 213 | 15.4 | 2.7 | 16 | 4 | 22 |
| 15.0 | 213 | 15.8 | 2.4 | 16 | 6 | 23 |
| 15.5 | 213 | 15.9 | 2.1 | 16 | 5 | 20 |
| 16.0 | 213 | 16.1 | 2.0 | 16 | 7 | 21 |
| 16.5 | 213 | 16.4 | 2.1 | 16 | 10 | 21 |
| 17.0 | 213 | 16.7 | 2.1 | 17 | 11 | 22 |
| 17.5 | 188 | 16.9 | 2.1 | 17 | 12 | 24 |
| 18.0 | 76 | 16.8 | 2.0 | 17 | 12 | 21 |

**Table D21    Speed of limb movement—plate tapping (#/20 sec)**

| Age (years) | N | M | SD | Median | Minimum | Maximum |
|---|---|---|---|---|---|---|
| 12.5 | 135 | 75.1 | 7.6 | 74 | 57 | 98 |
| 13.0 | 213 | 76.6 | 7.8 | 76 | 58 | 101 |
| 13.5 | 213 | 79.7 | 8.2 | 80 | 56 | 105 |
| 14.0 | 213 | 83.2 | 8.1 | 83 | 58 | 108 |
| 14.5 | 213 | 86.6 | 8.4 | 87 | 60 | 108 |
| 15.0 | 213 | 89.0 | 8.3 | 90 | 62 | 109 |
| 15.5 | 213 | 91.0 | 8.2 | 91 | 67 | 112 |
| 16.0 | 213 | 92.5 | 8.2 | 93 | 68 | 115 |
| 16.5 | 213 | 93.6 | 8.5 | 94 | 71 | 116 |
| 17.0 | 213 | 94.7 | 8.5 | 95 | 74 | 115 |
| 17.5 | 188 | 95.5 | 8.8 | 95 | 75 | 117 |
| 18.0 | 78 | 95.6 | 9.4 | 96 | 76 | 119 |

**Table D22   Running speed—shuttle run (sec)**

| Age (years) | N | M | SD | Median | Minimum | Maximum |
|---|---|---|---|---|---|---|
| 12.5 | 137 | 22.9 | 1.6 | 22.9 | 19.4 | 27.8 |
| 13.0 | 210 | 22.9 | 1.6 | 22.8 | 19.4 | 27.5 |
| 13.5 | 210 | 22.5 | 1.5 | 22.3 | 18.3 | 26.2 |
| 14.0 | 210 | 22.2 | 1.5 | 21.9 | 18.3 | 27.1 |
| 14.5 | 210 | 21.8 | 1.5 | 21.7 | 18.3 | 27.0 |
| 15.0 | 210 | 21.6 | 1.4 | 21.6 | 17.9 | 26.7 |
| 15.5 | 210 | 21.5 | 1.4 | 21.4 | 18.5 | 26.5 |
| 16.0 | 210 | 21.3 | 1.4 | 21.1 | 18.2 | 26.5 |
| 16.5 | 210 | 21.1 | 1.4 | 21.0 | 18.3 | 26.6 |
| 17.0 | 210 | 20.9 | 1.4 | 20.8 | 17.8 | 26.7 |
| 17.5 | 185 | 20.8 | 1.3 | 20.7 | 17.1 | 25.2 |
| 18.0 | 73 | 20.9 | 1.2 | 20.9 | 17.9 | 23.9 |

**Table D23   Flexibility—sit and reach (cm)**

| Age (years) | N | M | SD | Median | Minimum | Maximum |
|---|---|---|---|---|---|---|
| 12.5 | 140 | 18.8 | 5.5 | 19 | 3 | 34 |
| 13.0 | 218 | 18.8 | 5.6 | 19 | 2 | 34 |
| 13.5 | 218 | 19.5 | 5.8 | 20 | 2 | 34 |
| 14.0 | 218 | 20.2 | 5.9 | 20 | 3 | 28 |
| 14.5 | 218 | 20.9 | 6.0 | 21 | 5 | 42 |
| 15.0 | 218 | 21.5 | 6.1 | 21 | 5 | 42 |
| 15.5 | 218 | 22.2 | 6.3 | 22 | 6 | 42 |
| 16.0 | 218 | 23.0 | 6.5 | 23 | 4 | 43 |
| 16.5 | 218 | 23.6 | 6.9 | 24 | 3 | 45 |
| 17.0 | 218 | 24.0 | 7.0 | 24 | 3 | 46 |
| 17.5 | 193 | 24.7 | 7.2 | 25 | 4 | 47 |
| 18.0 | 78 | 24.5 | 7.4 | 25 | 11 | 39 |

# Appendix E

## Number of Subjects and Estimated Velocities for Size and Performance Measurements at 6-Month Intervals From 13.0 to 17.5 Years

**Table E1  Weight (kg/year)**

| Age (years) | N | M | Median |
|---|---|---|---|
| 13.0 | 171 | 4.3 | 3.9 |
| 13.5 | 274 | 5.1 | 4.9 |
| 14.0 | 274 | 5.8 | 5.8 |
| 14.5 | 274 | 6.2 | 6.2 |
| 15.0 | 274 | 6.3 | 6.0 |
| 15.5 | 274 | 6.0 | 6.0 |
| 16.0 | 274 | 5.3 | 5.2 |
| 16.5 | 274 | 4.4 | 4.2 |
| 17.0 | 245 | 3.5 | 3.4 |
| 17.5 | 103 | 2.4 | 2.4 |

**Table E2    Height (cm/year)**

| Age (years) | N | M | Median |
|---|---|---|---|
| 13.0 | 172 | 5.4 | 5.1 |
| 13.5 | 276 | 6.2 | 6.0 |
| 14.0 | 276 | 7.3 | 7.4 |
| 14.5 | 276 | 7.9 | 8.0 |
| 15.0 | 276 | 7.6 | 7.6 |
| 15.5 | 276 | 6.2 | 6.3 |
| 16.0 | 276 | 4.4 | 4.2 |
| 16.5 | 276 | 3.0 | 2.7 |
| 17.0 | 247 | 2.2 | 1.9 |
| 17.5 | 104 | 1.5 | 1.3 |

**Table E3    Sitting height (cm/year)**

| Age (years) | N | M | Median |
|---|---|---|---|
| 13.0 | 167 | 2.4 | 2.3 |
| 13.5 | 271 | 2.9 | 3.0 |
| 14.0 | 271 | 3.6 | 3.6 |
| 14.5 | 271 | 4.0 | 4.0 |
| 15.0 | 271 | 3.9 | 3.9 |
| 15.5 | 271 | 3.5 | 3.3 |
| 16.0 | 271 | 2.7 | 2.7 |
| 16.5 | 271 | 2.0 | 1.8 |
| 17.0 | 244 | 1.4 | 1.3 |
| 17.5 | 104 | 1.0 | 0.9 |

**Table E4    Leg length (cm/year)**

| Age (years) | N | M | Median |
|---|---|---|---|
| 13.0 | 167 | 3.0 | 3.0 |
| 13.5 | 271 | 3.2 | 3.3 |
| 14.0 | 271 | 3.6 | 3.7 |
| 14.5 | 271 | 3.9 | 3.8 |
| 15.0 | 271 | 3.6 | 3.6 |
| 15.5 | 271 | 2.7 | 2.7 |
| 16.0 | 271 | 1.7 | 1.6 |
| 16.5 | 271 | 1.0 | 0.9 |
| 17.0 | 244 | 0.7 | 0.7 |
| 17.5 | 104 | 0.5 | 0.4 |

**Table E5    Biacromial breadth (cm/year)**

| Age (years) | N | M | Median |
|---|---|---|---|
| 13.0 | 171 | 0.5 | 0.4 |
| 13.5 | 274 | 0.8 | 0.8 |
| 14.0 | 274 | 1.6 | 1.5 |
| 14.5 | 274 | 2.2 | 2.1 |
| 15.0 | 274 | 2.4 | 2.2 |
| 15.5 | 274 | 1.8 | 1.9 |
| 16.0 | 274 | 1.0 | 1.1 |
| 16.5 | 274 | 0.7 | 0.8 |
| 17.0 | 245 | 0.9 | 0.9 |
| 17.5 | 103 | 0.9 | 1.0 |

### Table E6   Chest breadth (cm/year)

| Age (years) | N | M | Median |
|---|---|---|---|
| 13.0 | 171 | 1.0 | 1.0 |
| 13.5 | 272 | 0.9 | 0.9 |
| 14.0 | 272 | 0.8 | 0.9 |
| 14.5 | 272 | 1.3 | 1.4 |
| 15.0 | 272 | 1.9 | 1.9 |
| 15.5 | 272 | 1.7 | 1.7 |
| 16.0 | 272 | 1.1 | 1.2 |
| 16.5 | 272 | 0.8 | 0.7 |
| 17.0 | 243 | 0.6 | 0.4 |
| 17.5 | 101 | 0.4 | 0.4 |

### Table E7   Biepicondylar humerus breadth (mm/year)

| Age (years) | N | M | Median |
|---|---|---|---|
| 13.0 | 163 | 3.7 | 3.3 |
| 13.5 | 265 | 2.6 | 2.1 |
| 14.0 | 265 | 0.9 | 1.5 |
| 14.5 | 265 | 1.8 | 2.1 |
| 15.0 | 265 | 4.1 | 3.9 |
| 15.5 | 265 | 3.6 | 3.0 |
| 16.0 | 265 | 1.0 | 1.0 |
| 16.5 | 265 | −0.4 | −0.4 |
| 17.0 | 239 | −0.6 | −0.5 |
| 17.5 | 102 | −0.9 | −1.0 |

**Table E8    Bicondylar femur breadth (mm/year)**

| Age (years) | N | M | Median |
|---|---|---|---|
| 13.0 | 168 | 2.6 | 2.9 |
| 13.5 | 267 | 2.0 | 2.0 |
| 14.0 | 267 | 2.0 | 2.0 |
| 14.5 | 267 | 2.5 | 2.8 |
| 15.0 | 267 | 3.0 | 2.8 |
| 15.5 | 267 | 1.3 | 1.0 |
| 16.0 | 267 | −1.6 | −1.1 |
| 16.5 | 267 | −1.4 | −0.9 |
| 17.0 | 240 | 0.4 | 0.0 |
| 17.5 | 99 | 1.0 | 1.2 |

**Table E9    Chest circumference inspiration (cm/year)**

| Age (years) | N | M | Median |
|---|---|---|---|
| 13.0 | 166 | 2.8 | 2.7 |
| 13.5 | 270 | 3.5 | 3.4 |
| 14.0 | 270 | 4.2 | 4.1 |
| 14.5 | 270 | 4.7 | 4.7 |
| 15.0 | 270 | 4.9 | 4.7 |
| 15.5 | 270 | 4.3 | 4.4 |
| 16.0 | 270 | 3.5 | 3.6 |
| 16.5 | 270 | 3.1 | 3.1 |
| 17.0 | 241 | 2.8 | 2.8 |
| 17.5 | 104 | 1.8 | 1.9 |

**Table E10   Flexed arm circumference (cm/year)**

| Age (years) | N | M | Median |
|---|---|---|---|
| 13.0 | 169 | 0.6 | 0.7 |
| 13.5 | 271 | 0.9 | 1.0 |
| 14.0 | 271 | 1.3 | 1.2 |
| 14.5 | 271 | 1.6 | 1.5 |
| 15.0 | 271 | 1.6 | 1.5 |
| 15.5 | 271 | 1.5 | 1.4 |
| 16.0 | 271 | 1.5 | 1.4 |
| 16.5 | 271 | 1.2 | 1.0 |
| 17.0 | 242 | 0.7 | 0.8 |
| 17.5 | 102 | 0.2 | 0.4 |

**Table E11   Thigh circumference (cm/year)**

| Age (years) | N | M | Median |
|---|---|---|---|
| 13.0 | 168 | 0.8 | 0.9 |
| 13.5 | 269 | 1.5 | 1.5 |
| 14.0 | 269 | 2.7 | 2.4 |
| 14.5 | 269 | 2.6 | 2.5 |
| 15.0 | 269 | 1.7 | 1.9 |
| 15.5 | 269 | 1.7 | 1.9 |
| 16.0 | 269 | 2.3 | 2.1 |
| 16.5 | 269 | 2.2 | 2.1 |
| 17.0 | 241 | 1.7 | 1.8 |
| 17.5 | 101 | 1.3 | 0.9 |

**Table E12    Calf circumference (cm/year)**

| Age (years) | N | M | Median |
|---|---|---|---|
| 13.0 | 167 | 0.6 | 0.5 |
| 13.5 | 270 | 1.1 | 1.0 |
| 14.0 | 270 | 1.5 | 1.5 |
| 14.5 | 270 | 1.6 | 1.5 |
| 15.0 | 270 | 1.6 | 1.5 |
| 15.5 | 270 | 1.2 | 1.4 |
| 16.0 | 270 | 0.8 | 0.9 |
| 16.5 | 270 | 0.8 | 0.8 |
| 17.0 | 242 | 0.9 | 0.9 |
| 17.5 | 103 | 0.7 | 0.9 |

**Table E13    Triceps skinfold (log units/year)**

| Age (years) | N | M | Median |
|---|---|---|---|
| 13.0 | 167 | 3.3 | 2 |
| 13.5 | 268 | 1.3 | 1 |
| 14.0 | 268 | −0.4 | 0 |
| 14.5 | 268 | −3.3 | −4 |
| 15.0 | 268 | −6.3 | −5 |
| 15.5 | 268 | −9.3 | −10 |
| 16.0 | 268 | −14.2 | −12 |
| 16.5 | 268 | −10.0 | −7 |
| 17.0 | 240 | 3.1 | 0 |
| 17.5 | 101 | 11.3 | 9 |

**Table E14   Subscapular skinfold (log units/year)**

| Age (years) | N | M | Median |
|---|---|---|---|
| 13.0 | 164 | 4.8 | 5 |
| 13.5 | 261 | 4.5 | 5 |
| 14.0 | 261 | 5.5 | 6 |
| 14.5 | 261 | 5.0 | 5 |
| 15.0 | 261 | 2.6 | 3 |
| 15.5 | 261 | 2.3 | 3 |
| 16.0 | 261 | 3.7 | 3 |
| 16.5 | 261 | 5.0 | 5 |
| 17.0 | 233 | 5.6 | 5 |
| 17.5 | 97 | 4.6 | 6 |


**Table E15   Suprailiac skinfold (log units/year)**

| Age (years) | N | M | Median |
|---|---|---|---|
| 13.0 | 165 | 11.5 | 11 |
| 13.5 | 266 | 11.9 | 12 |
| 14.0 | 266 | 11.8 | 11 |
| 14.5 | 266 | 10.0 | 9 |
| 15.0 | 266 | 7.7 | 8 |
| 15.5 | 266 | 7.7 | 8 |
| 16.0 | 266 | 8.3 | 8 |
| 16.5 | 266 | 4.0 | 3 |
| 17.0 | 237 | −2.9 | −1 |
| 17.5 | 101 | −8.4 | −8 |

**Table E16   Calf skinfold (log units/year)**

| Age (years) | N | M | Median |
|---|---|---|---|
| 13.0 | 168 | −1.8 | −1 |
| 13.5 | 271 | 4.2 | 5 |
| 14.0 | 271 | 13.7 | 9 |
| 14.5 | 271 | 8.2 | 5 |
| 15.0 | 271 | −5.4 | −3 |
| 15.5 | 271 | −10.7 | −10 |
| 16.0 | 271 | −12.2 | −12 |
| 16.5 | 271 | −15.3 | −14 |
| 17.0 | 242 | −18.5 | −18 |
| 17.5 | 103 | −22.0 | −22 |

**Table E17   Static strength—arm pull (kg/year)**

| Age (years) | N | M | Median |
|---|---|---|---|
| 13.0 | 140 | 5.6 | 4.9 |
| 13.5 | 219 | 6.5 | 6.1 |
| 14.0 | 219 | 9.0 | 8.6 |
| 14.5 | 219 | 11.2 | 10.5 |
| 15.0 | 219 | 11.9 | 11.9 |
| 15.5 | 219 | 10.8 | 10.3 |
| 16.0 | 219 | 8.7 | 8.6 |
| 16.5 | 219 | 7.2 | 7.2 |
| 17.0 | 194 | 7.0 | 6.7 |
| 17.5 | 79 | 6.5 | 6.5 |

**Table E18    Explosive strength—vertical jump (cm/year)**

| Age (years) | N | M | Median |
|---|---|---|---|
| 13.0 | 141 | 2.3 | 2.7 |
| 13.5 | 222 | 2.8 | 2.6 |
| 14.0 | 222 | 3.2 | 3.2 |
| 14.5 | 222 | 4.0 | 3.9 |
| 15.0 | 222 | 4.7 | 4.5 |
| 15.5 | 222 | 4.5 | 4.3 |
| 16.0 | 222 | 4.1 | 3.9 |
| 16.5 | 222 | 3.3 | 3.4 |
| 17.0 | 197 | 2.0 | 2.1 |
| 17.5 | 81 | 1.5 | 1.4 |

**Table E19    Functional strength—bent arm hang (sec/year)**

| Age (years) | N | M | Median |
|---|---|---|---|
| 13.0 | 137 | 1.4 | 2.2 |
| 13.5 | 217 | 2.1 | 1.4 |
| 14.0 | 217 | 3.1 | 3.0 |
| 14.5 | 217 | 4.2 | 3.7 |
| 15.0 | 217 | 5.5 | 4.2 |
| 15.5 | 217 | 5.7 | 5.5 |
| 16.0 | 217 | 4.4 | 3.8 |
| 16.5 | 217 | 1.6 | 0.8 |
| 17.0 | 192 | −1.1 | −0.1 |
| 17.5 | 80 | −1.0 | −1.4 |

Table E20    Trunk strength—leg lifts (#lifts/year)

| Age (years) | N | M | Median |
|---|---|---|---|
| 13.0 | 137 | 0.2 | 0.0 |
| 13.5 | 213 | 0.7 | 0.6 |
| 14.0 | 213 | 1.3 | 1.0 |
| 14.5 | 213 | 1.1 | 1.0 |
| 15.0 | 213 | 0.4 | 0.4 |
| 15.5 | 213 | 0.3 | 0.0 |
| 16.0 | 213 | 0.5 | 0.4 |
| 16.5 | 213 | 0.6 | 0.5 |
| 17.0 | 188 | 0.6 | 0.5 |
| 17.5 | 76 | 0.3 | 0.9 |

Table E21    Speed of limb movement—plate tapping (#taps/year)

| Age (years) | N | M | Median |
|---|---|---|---|
| 13.0 | 135 | 6.5 | 6.8 |
| 13.5 | 213 | 6.9 | 6.6 |
| 14.0 | 213 | 7.1 | 7.0 |
| 14.5 | 213 | 5.8 | 6.0 |
| 15.0 | 213 | 4.3 | 4.5 |
| 15.5 | 213 | 3.4 | 3.5 |
| 16.0 | 213 | 2.5 | 2.6 |
| 16.5 | 213 | 2.1 | 2.7 |
| 17.0 | 188 | 2.4 | 2.7 |
| 17.5 | 78 | 3.4 | 3.9 |

**Table E22    Running speed—shuttle run (sec/year)**

| Age (years) | N | M | Median |
|---|---|---|---|
| 13.0 | 137 | −0.7 | −0.7 |
| 13.5 | 210 | −0.7 | −0.6 |
| 14.0 | 210 | −0.7 | −0.7 |
| 14.5 | 210 | −0.6 | −0.5 |
| 15.0 | 210 | −0.3 | −0.3 |
| 15.5 | 210 | −0.3 | −0.2 |
| 16.0 | 210 | −0.4 | −0.4 |
| 16.5 | 210 | −0.3 | −0.3 |
| 17.0 | 185 | −0.4 | −0.2 |
| 17.5 | 73 | −0.5 | −0.3 |

*Note.* A negative velocity for the run indicates improved performance.

**Table E23    Flexibility—sit and reach (cm/year)**

| Age (years) | N | M | Median |
|---|---|---|---|
| 13.0 | 140 | 1.3 | 1.0 |
| 13.5 | 218 | 1.5 | 1.0 |
| 14.0 | 218 | 1.4 | 1.3 |
| 14.5 | 218 | 1.3 | 1.0 |
| 15.0 | 218 | 1.3 | 1.4 |
| 15.5 | 218 | 1.5 | 1.5 |
| 16.0 | 218 | 1.4 | 1.4 |
| 16.5 | 218 | 1.0 | 1.0 |
| 17.0 | 193 | 0.8 | 0.9 |
| 17.5 | 78 | 1.1 | 1.0 |

# References

Ahlberg, J.H., Nilson, E.N., & Welsh, J.L. (1967). The theory of splines and their applications. New York: Academic Press.

Asmussen, E. (1962). Muscular performance. In K. Rodahl & S.M. Horvath (Eds.), *Muscle as a tissue* (pp. 161-175). New York: McGraw-Hill.

Asmussen, E. (1973). Growth in muscular strength and power. In G.L. Rarick (Ed.), *Physical activity: Human growth and development* (pp. 60-79). New York: Academic Press.

Asmussen, E., & Heebøll-Nielsen, Kr. (1955). A dimensional analysis of performance and growth in boys. *Journal of Applied Physiology, 7*, 593-603.

Asmussen, E., & Heebøll-Nielsen, Kr. (1956). Physical performance and growth in children. Influence of age, sex and intelligence. *Journal of Applied Physiology, 8*, 371-380.

Baker, P.T., Hunt, E.E., Jr., & Sen, T. (1958). The growth and interrelations of skinfolds and brachial tissues in man. *American Journal of Physical Anthropology, 16*, 39-58.

Beunen, G., de Beul, G., Ostyn, M., Renson, R., Simons, J., & Van Gerven, D. (1978). Age of menarche and motor performance in girls aged 11 through 18. In J. Borms & M. Hebbelinck (Eds.), *Pediatric work physiology* (pp. 118-123). Basel: Karger.

Beunen, G., Ostyn, M., Renson, R., Simons, J., & Van Gerven, D. (1976). Skeletal maturation and physical fitness of girls aged 12 through 16. *Hermes* (Leuven), *10*, 445-457.

Beunen, G., Ostyn, M., Simons, J., Renson, R., & Van Gerven, D. (1980). Motorische vaardigheid, somatische ontwikkeling en biologische maturiteit. *Geneeskunde en Sport, 13*, 36-42.

Beunen, G., Ostyn, M., Simons, J., Renson, R., & Van Gerven, D. (1981). Chronological and biological age as related to physical fitness in boys 12 to 19 years. *Annals of Human Biology, 8*, 321-331.

Beunen, G., Simons, J., Renson, R., Van Gerven, D., & Ostyn, M. (1980). Growth curves for anthropometric and motor components. In M. Ostyn, J. Simons, G. Beunen, R. Renson, & D. Van Gerven (Eds.), *Somatic and motor development of Belgian secondary schoolboys. Norms and standards* (pp. 49-71). Leuven: Leuven University Press.

Bielicki, T., Koniarek, J., & Malina, R.M. (1984). Interrelationships among certain measures of growth and maturation rate in boys during adolescence. *Annals of Human Biology, 11*, 201-210.

Billewicz, W.Z., Fellowes, H.M., & Thomson, A.M. (1981). Pubertal changes in boys and girls in Newcastle upon Tyne. *Annals of Human Biology, 8*, 211-219.

Bjorntorp, P. (1985). Obesity and the risk of cardiovascular disease. *Annals of Clinical Research, 17*, 3-9.

Boas, F. (1892). The growth of children. *Science, 19-20*, 256-257, 281-282, 351-352.

Boas, F. (1932). Studies in growth. *Human Biology, 4*, 307-350.

Bock, R.D., & Thissen, D. (1980). Statistical problems in fitting individual growth curves. In F.E. Johnston, A.F. Roche, & C. Susanne (Eds.), *Human physical growth and maturation: Methodologies and factors* (pp. 265-290). New York: Plenum.

Bouchard, C. (1966). Les differences individuelles en force musculaire statique. *Mouvement, 1,* 49-66.

Bouchard, C., & Malina, R.M. (1983). Genetics of physiological fitness and motor performance. *Exercise and Sport Science Reviews, 11,* 306-339.

Branta, C., Haubenstricker, J., & Seefeldt, V. (1984). Age changes in motor skills during childhood and adolescence. *Exercise and Sport Science Reviews, 12,* 467-520.

Carron, A.V., Aitken, E.J., & Bailey, D.A. (1977). The relationship of menarche to the growth and development of strength. In H. Lavallee & R.J. Shephard (Eds.), *Frontiers of activity and child health* (pp. 139-143). Quebec: Editions du Pelican.

Carron, A.V., & Bailey, D.A. (1974). Strength development in boys from 10 through 16 years. *Monographs of the Society for Research in Child Development, 39* (Serial No. 157).

Cheek, D.B. (1968). *Human growth.* Philadelphia: Lea & Febiger.

Chumlea, W.C. (1982). Physical growth in adolescence. In B.D. Wolman (Ed.), *Handbook of developmental psychology* (pp. 471-485). Englewood Cliffs, NJ: Prentice-Hall.

Clarke, H.H. (1971). *Physical and motor tests in the Medford boys' growth study.* Englewood Cliffs, NJ: Prentice-Hall.

Cunningham, D.A., Paterson, D.H., Blimkie, C.J.R., & Donner, A.P. (1984). Development of cardiorespiratory function in circumpubertal boys: A longitudinal study. *Journal of Applied Physiology, 56,* 302-307.

Deming, J. (1957). Application of the Gompertz curve to the observed pattern of growth in length of 48 individual boys and girls during the adolescent cycle of growth. *Human Biology, 29,* 83-122.

Dimock, H.S. (1937). *Rediscovering the adolescent.* New York: Association Press.

Ellis, J.D., Carron, A.V., & Bailey, D.A. (1975). Physical performance in boys from 10 through 16 years. *Human Biology, 47,* 263-281.

Espenschade, A. (1940). Motor performance in adolescence including the study of relationships with measures of physical growth and maturity. *Monographs of the Society for Research in Child Development, 5* (Serial No. 24).

Espenschade, A. (1960). Motor development. In W.R. Johnson (Ed.), *Science and medicine of exercise and sports* (pp. 419-439). New York: Harper.

Falkner, F., & Tanner, J.M. (Eds.). (1986). *Human growth. Volume 2. Postnatal growth, neurobiology.* New York: Plenum.

Faust, M.S. (1977). Somatic development of adolescent girls. *Monographs of the Society for Research in Child Development, 42* (Serial No. 169).

Fischbein, S. (1977). Intra-pair similarity in physical growth of monozygotic and of dizygotic twins during puberty. *Annals of Human Biology, 4,* 417-430.

Goldstein, H. (1978). Sampling for growth studies. In F. Falkner & J.M. Tanner (Eds.), *Human growth. Volume 1. Principles and prenatal growth* (pp. 183-208). New York: Plenum.

Hansman, C.F., & Maresh, M.M. (1961). A longitudinal study of skeletal maturation. *American Journal of Diseases of Children, 101,* 305-321.

Haubenstricker, J.L., & Seefeldt, V.D. (1986). Acquisition of motor skills during childhood. In V. Seefeldt (Ed.), *Physical activity and well-being* (pp. 41-102). Reston, VA: AAHPERD.

Hauspie, R.C., Wachholder, A., Baron, G., Cantraine, F., Susanne, C., & Graffar, M. (1980). A comparative study of the fit of four different functions to longitudinal data of growth in height of Belgian girls. *Annals of Human Biology, 7,* 347-358.

Johnston, F.E., Hamill, P.V.V., & Lemeshow, S. (1974). Skinfold thickness of youths 12-17 years. *United States Vital and Health Statistics* (Series 11, No. 132). Washington, DC: U.S. Government Printing Office.

Jones, H.E. (1944). The development of physical abilities. In N.B. Henry (Ed.), *The forty-third yearbook of the national society for the study of education. Part I. Adolescence* (pp. 100-122). Chicago: University of Chicago, Department of Education.

Jones, H.E. (1949). *Motor performance and growth: A developmental study of static dynamometric strength.* Berkeley: University of California Press.

Kemper, H.C.G. (Ed.). (1985). *Growth, health, and fitness of teenagers.* Basel: Karger.

Kemper, H.C.G., Storm-van Essen, L., & Verschuur, R. (1985). Height, weight and height velocity. In H.C.G. Kemper (Ed.), *Growth, health, and fitness of teenagers* (pp. 66-80). Basel: Karger.

Largo, R.H., Gasser, Th., Prader, A., Stuetzle, W., & Huber, P.J. (1978). Analysis of the adolescent growth spurt using smoothing spline functions. *Annals of Human Biology, 5,* 421-434.

Lestrel, P.E., & Brown, H.D. (1976). Fourier analysis of adolescent growth of the vault: A longitudinal study. *Human Biology, 48,* 517-528.

Lindgren, G. (1978). Growth of children with early, average and late ages of peak height velocity. *Annals of Human Biology, 5,* 253-267.

Malina, R.M. (1974). Adolescent changes in size, build, composition and performance. *Human Biology, 46,* 117-131.

Malina, R.M. (1978). Adolescent growth and maturation: Selected aspects of current research. *Yearbook of Physical Anthropology, 21,* 63-94.

Malina, R.M. (1980). Growth, strength, and physical performance. In G.A. Stull (Ed.), *Encyclopedia of physical education, fitness and sports: Training, environment, nutrition and fitness* (pp. 443-470). Salt Lake City: Brighton.

Malina, R.M. (1982). Physical growth and maturity characteristics of young athletes. In R.A. Magill, M.J. Ash, & F.L. Smoll (Eds.), *Children in sport* (pp. 73-96). Champaign, IL: Human Kinetics.

Malina, R.M. (1983). Menarche in athletes: A synthesis and hypothesis. *Annals of Human Biology, 10,* 1-24.

Malina, R.M. (1986a). Growth of muscle tissue and muscle mass. In F. Falkner & J.M. Tanner (Eds.), *Human growth. Volume 2. Postnatal growth, neurobiology* (pp. 77-99). New York: Plenum.

Malina, R.M. (1986b). Genetics of motor development and performance. In R.M. Malina & C. Bouchard (Eds.), *Sport and human genetics* (pp. 23-58). Champaign, IL: Human Kinetics.

Malina, R.M. (1986c). Energy expenditure and physical activity during childhood and youth. In A. Demirjian (Ed.), *Human growth: A multidisciplinary review* (pp. 215-225). London: Taylor & Francis.

Malina, R.M. (1988a). Biological maturity status of young athletes. In R.M. Malina (Ed.), *Young athletes: Biological, psychological, and educational perspectives.* Champaign, IL: Human Kinetics.

Malina, R.M. (1988b). Competitive youth sports and biological maturation. In E. Brown (Ed.), *Competitive sports for children and youths: An overview of research and issues* (pp. 227-245). Champaign, IL: Human Kinetics.

Malina, R.M. (in press). Growth and maturation of young athletes: Biological and social considerations. In F.L. Smoll, R.A. Magill, & M.A Ash (Eds.), *Children in sport* (3rd ed.). Champaign, IL: Human Kinetics.

Malina, R.M., & Johnston, F.E. (1967). Significance of age, sex, and maturity differences in upper arm composition. *Research Quarterly, 38*, 219-230.

Marshall, W.A. (1974). Interrelationships of skeletal maturation, sexual development and somatic growth in man. *Annals of Human Biology, 1*, 29-40.

Marshall, W.A., & Tanner, J.M. (1986). Puberty. In F. Falkner & J.M. Tanner (Eds.), *Human growth. Volume 2. Postnatal growth, neurobiology* (pp. 171-209). New York: Plenum.

Marubini, E., Resele, L.F., Tanner, J.M., & Whitehouse, R.H. (1972). The fit of Gompertz and logistic curves to longitudinal data during adolescence on height, sitting height and biacromial diameter in boys and girls of the Harpenden Growth Study. *Human Biology, 44*, 511-524.

Merni, F., Balboni, M., Bargellini, S., & Menegatti, G. (1981). Differences in males and females in joint movement range during growth. In J. Borms, M. Hebbelinck, & A. Venerando (Eds.), *The female athlete* (pp. 168-175). Basel: Karger.

Metheny, E. (1941). The present status of strength testing for children of elementary school and preschool age. *Research Quarterly, 12*, 115-130.

Mirwald, R.L., & Bailey, D.A. (1986). *Maximal aerobic power: A longitudinal analysis*. London, Ontario: Sports Synamics.

Nicolson, A.B., & Hanley, C. (1953). Indices of physiological maturity: Derivation and interrelationships. *Child Development, 24*, 3-38.

Ostyn, M., Simons, J., Beunen, G., Renson, R., & Van Gerven, D. (Eds.). (1980). *Somatic and motor development of Belgian secondary schoolboys. Norms and standards*. Leuven: Leuven University Press.

Pařízková, J. (1976). Growth and growth velocity of lean body mass and fat in adolescent boys. *Pediatric Research, 10*, 647-650.

Parnell, R.W. (1958). *Behaviour and physique. An introduction to practical and applied somatometry*. London: Arnold.

Preece, M.A., & Baines, M.J. (1978). A new family of mathematical models describing the human growth curve. *Annals of Human Biology, 5*, 1-24.

Reiter, E.O., & Grumbach, M.M. (1982). Neuroendocrine control mechanisms and the onset of puberty. *Annual Review of Physiology, 44*, 595-613.

Renson, R., Beunen, G., Van Gerven, D., Simons, J., & Ostyn, M. (1980). Description of motor ability tests and anthropometric measurements. In M. Ostyn, J. Simons, G. Beunen, R. Renson, & D. Van Gerven, *Somatic and motor development of Belgian secondary schoolboys. Norms and standards* (pp. 24-44). Leuven: Leuven University Press.

Rivet, P. (1912). Entente internationale pour l'unification des mesures anthropométriques sur le vivant. *L'anthropologie, 23*, 623-627.

Roche, A.F. (1974). Differential timing of maximum length increments among bones within individuals. *Human Biology, 46*, 145-157.

Roche, A.F., & Lewis, A.B. (1974). Sex differences in the elongation of the cranial base during pubescence. *Angle Orthodontist, 44*, 279-294.

Roede, M.J., & Van't Hof, M.A. (1979). Variability in growth acceleration patterns. In B. Prahl-Andersen, C.J. Kowalski, & P. Heydendael (Eds.), *A mixed-longitudinal interdisciplinary study of growth and development* (pp. 459-463). New York: Academic Press.

Roy, M.P. (1972). Evolution clinique de la puberte du garçon. In *Compte rendu de la XI$_e$ reunion des equipes chargees des etudes sur la croissance et le developpement de l'enfant normal* (pp. 185-190). Paris: Centre International de l'Enfance.

Rutenfranz, J., Andersen, K., Seliger, V., Ilmarinen, J., Klimmer, F., Kylian, H., Rutenfranz, M., & Ruppel, M. (1982). Maximal aerobic power affected by maturation and body growth during childhood and adolescence. *European Journal of Pediatrics,* **139,** 106-112.

Shuttleworth, F.K. (1937). Sexual maturation and the physical growth of girls aged six to nineteen. *Monographs of the Society for Research in Child Development,* **2** (Serial No. 12).

Simons, J., Beunen, G., Ostyn, M., Renson, R., Swalus, P., Van Gerven, D., & Willems, E. (1969). Construction d'une batterie de tests d'aptitude motrice pour garçons de 12 à 19 ans, par la méthode de l'analyse factorielle. *Kinanthropologie,* **1,** 323-362.

Simons, J., Beunen, G., Renson, R., Van Gerven, D., & Ostyn, M. (1980a). The mixed-longitudinal growth study. In M. Ostyn, J. Simons, G. Beunen, R. Renson, & D. Van Gerven (Eds.), *Somatic and motor development of Belgian secondary schoolboys. Norms and standards* (pp. 11-23). Leuven: Leuven University Press.

Simons, J., Beunen, G., Renson, R., Van Gerven, D., & Ostyn, M. (1980b). Norm scales for anthropometric measurements and motor fitness. In M. Ostyn, J. Simons, G. Beunen, R. Renson, & D. Van Gerven (Eds.), *Somatic and motor development of Belgian secondary schoolboys. Norms and standards* (pp. 72-100). Leuven: Leuven University Press.

Singh, R. (1976). A longitudinal study of the growth of trunk surface area measured by planimeter on standard somatotype photographs. *Annals of Human Biology,* **3,** 181-186.

Sizonenko, P.C. (1978). Endocrinology in preadolescents and adolescents. I. Hormonal changes during normal puberty. *American Journal of Diseases of Children,* **132,** 704-712. ,

Skład, M. (1977). The rate of growth and maturing of twins. *Acta Geneticae, Medicae et Gemellologiae,* **26,** 221-237.

Stern, M.P., & Haffner, S.M. (1986). Body fat distribution and hyperinsulinemia as risk factors for diabetes and cardiovascular disease. *Arteriosclerosis,* **6,** 123-130.

Stolz, H.R., & Stolz, L.M. (1951). *Somatic development of adolescent boys.* New York: Macmillan.

Tanner, J.M. (1951). Some notes on the reporting of growth data. *Human Biology,* **23,** 93-159.

Tanner, J.M. (1962). *Growth at adolescence* (2nd ed.). Oxford: Blackwell.

Tanner, J.M. (1970). Physical growth. In P.H. Mussen (Ed.), *Carmichael's manual of child psychology. Volume 1* (pp. 77-155). New York: Wiley.

Tanner, J.M. (1978). *Foetus into man: Physical growth from conception to maturity.* London: Open Books.

Tanner, J.M. (1981). *A history of the study of human growth.* London: Cambridge University Press.

Tanner, J.M., Hughes, P.C.R., & Whitehouse, R.H. (1981). Radiographically determined widths of bone muscle and fat in the upper arm and calf from age 3-18 years. *Annals of Human Biology,* **8,** 495-517.

Tanner, J.M., & Whitehouse, R.H. (1975). Revised standards for triceps and subscapular skinfolds in British children. *Archives of Disease in Childhood,* **50,** 142-145.

Tanner, J.M., Whitehouse, R.H., Marubini, E., & Resele, L.F. (1976). The adolescent growth spurt of boys and girls of the Harpenden Growth Study. *Annals of Human Biology*, **3**, 109-126.

Tanner, J.M., Whitehouse, R.H., & Takaishi, M. (1966). Standards from birth to maturity for height, weight, height velocity and weight velocity. *Archives of Disease in Childhood*, **41**, 454-471, 613-635.

Taranger, J., Engstrom, I., Lichtenstein, H., & Svennberg-Redegren, I. (1976). Somatic pubertal development. *Acta Paediatrica Scandinavica* (Suppl. 258), 121-135.

Thissen, D., Bock, R.D., Wainer, H., & Roche, A.F. (1976). Individual growth in stature: A comparison of four growth studies in the U.S.A. *Annals of Human Biology*, **3**, 529-542.

Ungerer, D. (1973). Leistungs- und Belastungsfähigkeit im Kindes- und Jungendalter. *Schriftenreihe zur Praxis der Leibeserziehung und des Sports*. Schorndorf: Hofmann.

Van Druten, J.A.M. (1981). *A mathematical-statistical model for the analysis of cross-sectional serological data with respect to the epidemiology of malaria*. Unpublished doctoral dissertation, K.U. Nijmegen.

Van't Hof, M.A., Beunen, G., & Simons, J. *The selection of useful somatic measurements in a longitudinal growth study*. Manuscript submitted for publication.

Van't Hof, M.A., & Kowalski, C.J. (1979). Analysis of mixed-longitudinal data sets. In B. Prahl-Andersen, C.J. Kowalski, & S.P. Heydendael (Eds.), *A mixed-longitudinal interdisciplinary study of growth and development* (pp. 161-172). New York: Academic Press.

Van't Hof, M.A., Roede, J.J., & Kowalski, C.J. (1976). Estimation of growth velocities from individual longitudinal data. *Growth*, **40**, 217-240.

Van't Hof, M.A., Roede, J.J., & Kowalski, C.J. (1977). A mixed longitudinal data analysis model. *Human Biology*, **49**, 165-179.

Van't Hof, M.A., Simons, J., & Beunen, G. (1980). Data quality evaluation and data processing. In M. Ostyn, J. Simons, G. Beunen, R. Renson, & D. Van Gerven (Eds.), *Somatic and motor development of Belgian secondary schoolboys. Norms and standards* (pp. 45-48). Leuven: Leuven University Press.

Veling, S.H.J., & Van't Hof, M.A. (1980). Data quality control methods in longitudinal studies. In M. Ostyn, G. Beunen, & J. Simons (Eds.), *Kinanthropometry II* (pp. 436-442). Baltimore: University Park Press.

Wafelbakker, F. (1969). Adolescent growth spurt in relation to age and maturation. In J. Kral & V. Novotny (Eds.), *Physical fitness and its laboratory assessment* (pp. 49-52). Prague: Universitas Carolina Pragensis.

1488